W9-DEU-368

***Other books by* Laurie Blum:**

FREE MONEY FOR FOREIGN STUDY

FREE MONEY FOR GRADUATE STUDY

FREE MONEY FOR HUMANITIES STUDENTS

FREE MONEY FOR HUMANITIES & SOCIAL SCIENCES

FREE MONEY FOR MATHEMATICS & NATURAL SCIENCES

FREE MONEY FOR PEOPLE IN THE ARTS

FREE MONEY FOR PROFESSIONAL STUDIES

FREE MONEY FOR SCIENCE STUDENTS

FREE MONEY FOR SMALL BUSINESSES & ENTREPRENEURS

FREE MONEY FOR UNDERGRADUATE STUDY

HOW TO GET FEDERAL GRANTS

HOW TO INVEST IN REAL ESTATE USING FREE MONEY

Laurie Blum's

FREE MONEY

for Private Schools

A Fireside Book
Published by Simon & Schuster
New York London Toronto Sydney Tokyo Singapore

FIRESIDE
Simon & Schuster Building
Rockefeller Center
1230 Avenue of the Americas
New York, New York 10020

Copyright © 1992 by Laurie Blum

All rights reserved
including the right of reproduction
in whole or in part in any form.

FIRESIDE and colophon are registered trademarks
of Simon & Schuster Inc.

Designed by Christina M. Riley
Manufactured in the United States of America

1 3 5 7 9 10 8 6 4 2

Library of Congress Cataloging in Publication Data
is available

ISBN 0-671-74591-3

I would like to briefly but sincerely thank my "A Team," Christina, Erica, and Fori, as well as my wonderful editor Ed Walters, and of course Alan Kellock.

Contents

Foreword

by Paul Cummins
Headmaster, Crossroads School for Arts and Sciences

When the parents of today's adolescents were growing up, the term "private school" brought to mind the small, church-subsidized parochial school. Certainly large, well-established independent schools existed and had a long tradition in this country, but they were considered schools for the elite — out of the reach of most middle class families.

Over the last quarter century, three shifts have occurred in independent schools and also in how we think about independent schools. First, the education community has been considering, experimenting with, and implementing a wide variety of new ideas on how best to approach the education of our children. The "progressive" schools of the sixties and seventies are one of the forums in which much of this innovation has taken place, and is continuing.

Second, the public school system has been continuing to grapple with a host of challenges, including a widely expanding student population, reduced funding, an increased need to deal with the problems raised by changes in family structure, mixing of different cultures and different languages, increased crime, and above all an urgent need for funds. Some parents have responded to these challenges by fleeing from the public school system to smaller organizations, while others have responded by calling on the private institutions to assist in the solving of public problems through community outreach programs.

Finally, the independent schools themselves have moved increasingly from being elitist institutions for the upper classes to becoming socially alert institutions with active programs for financial assistance, strong programs for attracting and retaining minority children, and a commitment to multi-culturalism.

I am a founder and the Headmaster of Crossroads School for Arts and Sciences, a K-12 independent school in Santa Monica, California, founded in 1971. Crossroads is an example of this generation's independent school. We certainly talk with new parents and faculty about our academic successes and our arts and athletic programs. Crossroads received a U.S. Department of Education Award in 1984 for being one of sixty exemplary private schools in America, and we also maintain a highly competitive athletic program, plus one of the best high school string ensembles in the country. We talk with equal enthusiasm, however, about our required courses in Ethics and our award-winning Community Service program, our 20% minority enrollment, our community outreach programs with local area public schools, and our commitment to reserve 10% of our total operating budget for financial aid.

The school has been exciting to administer. While it is now beginning to approach (or at least imagine) financial maturity, it was originally founded on a shoestring. We are located in an industrial neighborhood, near a freeway, having acquired first one then another of the buildings as our funds became available and our student body expanded. Crossroads is far from the typical ivy-covered walls of the traditional private school, and our fresh approach can be seen daily in the diversity of our student body — both in their backgrounds and in their interests and pursuits.

The challenges facing the Crossroads parent body are typical for parents of independent school children. Tuition, fees, books and expenses are now more than $10,000 for secondary school students at Crossroads and nearly $8,000 for elementary school students. Quite frankly, a family in the Los Angeles area (where, as this is written in May of 1990, the typical mortgage payment is over $20,000 a year for a 3-bedroom home) needs to be making around $100,000 in gross income to be able to pay $10,000 for schooling without feeling some level of financial strain.

But we need and want families with a wider range of economic diversity in order to maintain the kind of interesting and widely varied student body that we want to have in the school. What are we, and the parents, to do?

Schools have increasingly expanded their financial aid programs to meet this need. While Crossroads gives a higher percentage of financial aid than most schools, we are beginning to find other schools increasing their aid to approach our level of 10% of the operating budget. Financial aid is competitive, however. We receive many more applications than we can meet with available funds. We find that we are often able to provide some sort of assistance for families earning less than $50,000 but that we usually cannot grant these families as much aid as they truly need in order to attend the school without straining the family finances to some degree. For families in the $50,000 to $100,000 income range, in the majority of cases, we simply cannot grant any financial aid.

Laurie Blum's *Free Money For Private Schools* is exactly what we have needed in order to be able to provide some assistance to the families to whom we cannot award adequate aid. We have found some sources of tuition financing at low interest rates. However, it is important to realize that there is a difference between a family with real need and one with a cash flow problem. Tuition financing will probably not provide much relief to the family with real need; what is needed for families are additional sources for financial aid. We have, in some rare cases (for students in the arts) become aware of possible outside funding sources. But we have never had available a comprehensive list of foundations and funding sources to which parents could be referred. That is what Laurie Blum's book provides.

Losing a talented and delightful student because funds are not available is devastating for the family but also painful for the school. By allowing us to help families find supplemental funds for their children's schooling, I feel that *Free Money For Private Schools* is providing a very real service for schools across the country like Crossroads, as well as for the countless families who will benefit from the information.

Introduction

Free Money for Private Schools is an important volume in my child care series. Currently, nearly five million children attend private schools for grades K to 12, and another 1.8 million are enrolled in private nursery schools. The parents of millions more would probably choose private schools over public schools if they could afford it. With private school education, parents are assured of helping their children escape the increasing deterioration of the quality of public education and the dangerous environments of many public schools.

Unfortunately, the cost of private school tuition is rapidly increasing, yet up until now there has been no resource guide to provide parents with sources of funds to help them better afford the costs of sending a child (or children) to private school. This book is intended to be such a resource guide and has been designed with an easy-to-use format to help parents of all income levels access the financial assistance they need to provide their children with the best education money can buy.

Free Money for Private Schools identifies thousands of sources for hundreds of thousands of dollars available to help parents pay for private schooling. The book includes information on funding available in all 50 states and covers both grants and scholarships tied to income levels, as well as those with no financial strings attached.

While writing this book, I was amazed to discover that in addition to private foundation and corporate grant sources, there were quite a few private schools (a sampling of which I have included in this book) that offer financial aid to middle class parents, based on the family's ability to shoulder the costs of the school's tuition. Thus, a family whose annual income is $50,000 could, in fact, receive some sort of financial aid. In addition, many private schools offer financial aid based on a student's hobby (e.g., debate), talent (e.g., music), or special ability (e.g., athletics).

With the rising costs of tuition and the declining ability of family income to cover costs of living, let alone expensive and often prohibitive private school tuitions, this is "good news." In today's shrinking economy and in a world where many families are now headed by a single parent, access to financial aid has become a necessity for many families if their children are to enjoy the benefits of a private school education.

Despite the limitations of space in this book, I have tried to cover as many areas as possible that will assist parents in being able to make the choice of whether or not to send their child to private school. This information covers private foundation support (including corporate/employee support, religious foundations, and foundation support based on extracurricular activities), as well as a random sampling of several private schools in each state that give generous financial aid to middle class students.

Overall, *Free Money for Private Schools* provides information on a wide cross-section of private foundation and corporate assistance available to middle class (and other) parents to help them meet the cost of a private school education.

This book is divided into four chapters:

1) "Corporate/Employee Scholarships";

2) "Special Population Funding";

3) "Private School Financial Aid"; and

4) "Miscellaneous Grants."

The chapter on "Special Population Funding" covers private school funding assistance available to children and families in special categories, including: American Indian families, developmentally disabled children, and children of migratory workers. This chapter also lists miscellaneous federal funding sources for special populations, including minority and disadvantaged students.

The chapter on "Miscellaneous Grants" lists a widely ranging array of assistance sources, including extracurricular scholarships, religious grants and private foundation grants.

Within each chapter, listings are arranged state-by-state to make this book as easy to use as possible. Check your state's listings in all four chapters to see which grants or programs apply to you. You'll find all the details that you need, including the funding parameters of each resource, an address and phone number to contact for further information (and application forms), the total amount and range of money that is awarded, the number of grants or loans given, and the average size of an award.

By the time this book is published, some of the information contained here will have changed. No reference book can be as up-to-date as the reader or author would like. Names, addresses, dollar amounts, telephone numbers, and other data are always in flux; however, most of the information will not have changed.

While reviewing this data, readers are advised to remember that funding sources are not without restrictions and that researching, applying for and receiving aid will take time, effort, diligence, and thought. You are going to have to identify the sources of aid for which you qualify and determine whether or not you fulfill geographic and other requirements. You are going to have to fill out applications. You may meet with rejection and frustration somewhere along this road. The odds, however, are in your favor that you will qualify for some sort of funding assistance.

Following is a concise, how-to guide to writing a grant proposal. Follow my instructions and you should be successful in obtaining some sort of financial assistance to help you afford private school education for your children. Good luck.

How to apply

Thousands of resources for financial aid to parents for private education of their elementary and secondary school age children exist throughout the country. Resources for this assistance include: private foundations, corporations/companies, and financial aid/scholarship programs offered directly by private schools. Applying for this aid is the challenging part and requires diligence, thought and organization.

First is the sorting out process or research/gathering phase. Look through each chapter of the book on a state-by-state basis and mark each potential assistance source. (Many resources only provide aid in their state of operations, excluding certain corporations whose operations may span more than one state). Pay close attention to the listed restrictions and qualifications, and eliminate from your list the resources least likely to assist you.

Then, politely contact each of your listed sources by mail or phone to verify all current information, such as address, telephone, name of the proper contact, and his/her title (in cases where the contact's name is not listed, begin your letter, "To Whom It May Concern"). At this time, you can also arrange to get a copy of the source's most current assistance guidelines, and an application form (if that is what is required). Use this opportunity to find out about any application deadlines and to ask where you are in the funding cycle (i.e., if there is no deadline, when would be the best time to apply; also, be sure to ask when awards will be announced and funds distributed). However, never "grill" or cross-examine the person you reach on the phone. Always be prepared to talk about why you are applying and what you are applying for — in case you ring through to the key decisionmaker, who decides on the spot to interview you!

Second is the application phase. In terms of private school assistance, most often you will be asked to submit a formal application (rather than a proposal). Usually the same material used for one application can be applied to most, if not all, of your other applications, with a little restructuring (making sure you answer each and every question as asked, appropriate to each application). Always be sure to read (and follow!) the instructions for completing the application.

Grant applications take time (and thought) to fill out, so make sure you give yourself enough time to do this before the application deadline. Filling out the application can be a lengthy process, because you may be required to write one or more essays. Often, what is required is a "statement of purpose" explaining what you will use the money for and sometimes explaining why you need the assistance for which you are applying. You may also need time to assemble required attachments, such as tax returns and other financial records. (Don't worry, you won't be penalized for having money in the bank.) You may also be required to include personal references. Be sure to get strong references. Call all of the people you plan to list, and ask them if they feel comfortable giving you or your child references. Remember, you have to convince the grantors to put money toward *your* child's education, perhaps instead of someone else's.

Be clear, concise and neat! You may very well prepare a top-notch application, but it won't look good if it's been prepared in a sloppy manner. Applications (and proposals) should always be typed and double-spaced. Make sure you keep a copy after you send off the original — I have learned the hard way that there is nothing worse than having the funding source be unable to find your application and your having to reconstruct it because you didn't keep a copy.

You should apply to a number of funding sources for grants and scholarships, as no one application is guaranteed to win an award. Although none of the sources listed in this book requires an application fee, the effort you will have to put in will probably limit you to no more than eight applications (if you are ambitious and want to apply to more than eight sources, go right ahead). Remember, the more sources you apply to, the greater your chances for success.

The following is an example of a typical corporate/employee grant application. This one happens to be for a non-profit organization, The Parent Connection, Inc., however, the form will be similar for you as an individual and is typical of the type of grant application you will be making.

TRW Employees CHarity Organization Grant Application

To: ☒ TRW Employees Charity Organization
One Space Park, Building S, Room 1420
Redondo Beach, California 90278

☐ Other TRW ECHO Unit (Offsite)

Dear Grant Applicant:

Please fill in this Grant Application, providing us with the best information you have available, to aid us in evaluating your request for funds. Include, if you wish, brochures and other supporting information but any omissions on this form may prevent consideration of your request.

Thank you
TRW ECHO Governing Board

(Please Print or Type)

1. LEGAL NAME OF ORGANIZATION
THE PARENT CONNECTION, INC.
2. ALSO KNOWN AS (OR FORMER NAME)

FOR ECHO USE ONLY

3. ADDRESS
3709 SAWTELLE BLVD. LOS ANGELES, CA 90066

4. TELEPHONE NUMBER (S)
(213) 823-7846
( )

5. IRS NUMBER (ATTACH CURRENT COPY OF 501(C)(3) CLEARANCE)
95-4115121

6. DATE ESTABLISHED
OCT 15, 1987

7. STAFF INFORMATION

CATEGORY	TOTAL NUMBER OF STAFF	AVERAGE HRS PER PERSON PER ~~MONTH~~ week	AVERAGE MONTHLY BUDGET
FULL TIME STAFF	2	40	see attached
PART TIME STAFF	10	4	
VOLUNTEERS	28	12	
BOARD MEMBERS	9	4	

8. TYPE OF SOCIAL SERVICES PROVIDED
Parental guidance classes for high-risk adult and teenage parents.

9. SUMMARIZE THE SOURCE OF ANNUAL FUNDING

FEE OR TUITIONS $ see attached
INDIVIDUALS $
UNITED WAY $
FOUNDATIONS $
CORPORATIONS $
GOVERNMENT $
ENDOWED INCOME $
OTHER (SPECIFY) $
TOTAL $

10. COPY OF CURRENT BUDGET ATTACHED (IF NONE - EXPLAIN)
attached

11. COPY OF LATEST CPA AUDIT REPORT ATTACHED (IF NONE - EXPLAIN)
attached (1988 is not complete)

12. PERCENT DISTRIBUTION OF FUNDS

FUND RAISING	25 %
ADMINISTRATION	15 %
DIRECT TO SOCIAL	60 %
	100%

13. DESCRIBE THE PURPOSE FOR WHICH THE FUNDS WILL BE USED, HOW IT WILL BENEFIT A SEGMENT OF THE COMMUNITY AND DESCRIPTION OF HOW THE PROJECT WILL BE CARRIED OUT.

Funds will be used to pay for low income, underprivileged parents and teenagers to attend our SKILLFUL PARENTING: BECAUSE LOVE IS NOT ENOUGH program. We receive referrals from the dependancy and juvenile courts weekly as well as the Social Welfare Department and attorneys for parents to take the training we provide. We are instrumental in keeping families together by offering a specialized training in the fundamentals of responsible parenting. The letter they receive at the completion of the training is used in court as evidence that they have received the training. Many children are returned to parents at the completion of these classes. Enclosed is more detailed information on our classes. (The program that we offer for teenagers at Camp Scott is called "Taking Charge."

AMOUNT REQUESTED $ $5000

14. PREPARER INFORMATION

A. Jayne Major
A. Jayne Major, PhD
TYPE NAME AND SIGN

Executive Director
TITLE OR POSITION

~~April 10,~~ 1989
DATE

15. DESCRIBE YOUR ORGANIZATION (Include purpose, services offerred, number of people served, fee structure, chronology of accomplishments and criteria used to measure success).

1. Our purpose is to educate parents and parents to be in themost important role that they will ever have, that of raising children.

2. See attached flier for classes and for program offered at Camp Scott.

3. We serve approximately 65 people weekly in our classes. We could train more parents with financial assistance.

4. Our fee structure is $200, $150, $100 or $50 per student. Most students pay per class rather than all at once.

5. See enclosed for chronology of accomplishments.

6. Criteria used to measure success is the completion of a study guide required for letter indicating that the parent has completed the course.

16. ARE THERE OTHER CHARITIES WITH SIMILAR OR OVERLAPPING SERVICES IN YOUR AREA? IF SO, IDENTITFY.

There are other agencies that offer parent education classes. Ours is the only one where we have a continuous enrollment policy and speciallize is the most problematic of families.

17. NAMES OF TRW EMPLOYEES EITHER PARTICIPATING IN PROGRAM OR BEING SERVED.

Chuck Merriman and his wife Elissa Merriman have completed our program. Other TRW employees are invited to avail themselves of this service.

18. LIST PREVIOUS GRANTS RECEIVED FROM TRW (ECHO or corporate contributions committee) FOR 5 YEARS.

No grants have been received from TRW before.

19. ADDITIONAL COMMENTS

Thank you for the charatible work that you do, and for considering this request.

Corporate/ Employee Programs

This chapter contains information on companies and corporations that provide funding through grants and scholarships to assist with the costs of private education. This assistance is offered to employees and their children directly, as well as to applicants on a non-employee basis who qualify under the company's giving guidelines. Generally, most companies and corporations offer assistance with schools located in their area of operations or in the area of their administrative headquarters.

As you will see from the following national listings, funding is available at the elementary and secondary levels. Some corporations offer cash grants directly to employees or other qualified applicants with no strings attached, while others offer support only on a matching fund basis; i.e., when your other funding sources can match dollar-for-dollar or on a percentage basis the amount of the grant given to you by the corporation.

Some corporate funders offer direct grants only to specific kinds of schools and other non-profit organizations. For example, your child's individual grant may become available as part of a larger application by a school (or other tax-exempt special interest group) to set up a scholarship or financial assistance program. Or, it may be that a corporate funder currently offers assistance at select schools in their general giving area (i.e., private schools for the learning disabled).

To pursue this type of assistance opportunity, it is best to check directly with the funder. Find out whom they fund and through which pertinent nonprofit groups and organizations. See if you can apply "through" the non-profit, or as part of a larger financial aid application.

CORPORATE/EMPLOYEE PROGRAMS

In many instances, corporate funders have set up assistance programs directly at the schools they fund, so while the monies are made available by the corporation, the application is made to and through the school. Finally, many corporations and companies give assistance only in certain areas of study (such as "Earth Sciences") or to special populations of students ("gifted students"). As always, when reviewing grant and financial assistance sources, make sure there is a "match" between your area of need and the corporation or company's qualifications for giving.

ALABAMA

Blount
Blount Foundation
4520 Executive Park Drive
Montgomery, AL 36116
(205) 244–4348

Description: One–half of education monies given to colleges, one–third given in matching grants; emphasis on state of Alabama, especially Montgomery area and Blount operating locations
$ Given: Of $680,000 corporate giving total, 25–30% designated for education
Contact: D. Joseph McInnes, President

Vulcan Materials Company
Vulcan Materials Company Foundation
P.O. Box 530187
Birmingham, AL 35253–0187
(205) 877–3229

Description: Awards for private pre–college education in states where company has operations; funding for a few national organizations
$ Given: Of $2,700,000 corporate giving total, 50–55% designated for education
Contact: Mary S. Russom, Community Affairs Representative

CALIFORNIA

American Honda Motor Company, Inc.
American Honda Foundation
P.O. Box 2205
Torrance, CA 90509–2205
(213) 781–4090

Description: National funding for scholarships and Gifted Student Program
$ Given: Of $775,000 corporate giving total, 50% designated for education
Contact: Kathryn A. Carey, Foundation Manager

Apple Computer, Inc.
Education Grants Program
Apple Community Affairs
20525 Mariani Avenue
MS 38J
Cupertino, CA 95014
(408) 974–2974

Description: National funding to support educational projects that use microcomputers to create new ways of learning and teaching; donated computer equipment constitutes the bulk of company gifts
$ Given: $7,250,000 corporate giving total; amount to education not specified
Contact: Andrea Gonzales, Program Officer, Education Grants

CORPORATE/EMPLOYEE PROGRAMS

The Clorox Company
Clorox Company Foundation
P.O. Box 24305
Oakland, CA 94623
(415) 271–7747

Description: One–third of education monies given to colleges; priority given to organizations located in Oakland, others eligible for assistance include those in San Francisco East Bay Area and in areas where Clorox has operating facilities
$ Given: Of $2,500,000 corporate giving total, 15–20% designated for education
Contact: Carmella H. Johnson, Contributions Manager

Hewlett–Packard Company
Hewlett–Packard Foundation
P.O. Box 10301
Palo Alto, CA 94303
(413) 857–3053

Description: Majority of support in the form of equipment grants to more than 100 colleges and universities; recipients located principally near operating locations; national organizations also funded
$ Given: $69,000,000 corporate giving total; amount to education not specified, but education is a top priority
Contact: Roderick Carlson, Director of Corporate Communications

Mattel
Mattel Foundation
5150 Rosecrans Avenue
Hawthorne, CA 90250
(213) 978–5477

Description: One–half of education monies awarded in the forms of matching gifts and scholarships; giving focused primarily in the Los Angeles area and in Southern California
$ Given: Of $1,000,000 corporate giving total, 30% designated for education
Contact: Janice Morimoto, Administrator

National Medical Enterprises
2700 Colorado Boulevard
P.O. Box 4070
Santa Monica, CA 90404
(213) 315–8215

Description: Funding provided principally to those located near corporate operating locations; national organizations also funded
$ Given: Of $2,800,000 corporate giving total, 15% designated for education
Contact: Dyanne M. Hayes, Director of Corporate Contributions

Occidental Petroleum Corporation
Occidental Petroleum Charitable Foundation
10889 Wilshire Boulevard
Los Angeles, CA 90024
(213) 879–1700

Description: 30% of education monies provided in form of matching funds; awards provided in communities where Occidental maintains facilities
$ Given: Of $1,215,053 corporate giving total, 35–40% designated for education
Contact: Evelyn C. Wong, Assistant Secretary & Treasurer

Southern California Edison Company
2244 Walnut Grove Avenue
P.O. Box 800
Rosemead, CA 91770
(818) 302–3841

Description: Funding focused primarily in the Southern California service area
$ Given: $4,000,000 corporate giving total; amount to education not specified
Contact: Rebecca S. Jones, Director, Charitable Contributions

Tandem Computers
10435 N. Tantau Avenue
Loc. 200–47
Cupertino, CA 95014–0709
(408) 285–4660

Description: Funding focused primarily near corporate headquarters in San Francisco and Santa Clara Valley, as well as in corporate operating areas
$ Given: $2,000,000 corporate giving total; amount to education not specified, but education is a top priority
Contact: Jennie Magid, Director, Corporate Grants

Teledyne
Teledyne Charitable Trust Foundation
1901 Avenue of the Stars
Los Angeles, CA 90067
(213) 277–3311

Description: Majority of education monies provided in the form of employee matching gifts to public and private secondary schools, and to institutions of higher education; funding focused primarily in areas where company operates facilities
$ Given: Of $1,520,298 corporate giving total, 5–55% designated for education
Contact: Gary A. Zitterbart, Treasurer

Times Mirror Company
Times Mirror Foundation
Times Mirror Square
Los Angeles, CA 90053
(213) 237–3936

Description: Awards to national organizations in Southern California and to those in communities served by corporate subsidiaries
$ Given: Of $10,008,761 corporate giving total, 25–30% designated for education
Contact: Stephen C. Meier, Secretary; or Cassandra Malry, Manager of Corporate Relations

CONNECTICUT

AMAX, Inc.
AMAX Foundation
AMAX Center
55 Railroad Avenue
Greenwich, CT 06836
(203) 629–6901

Description: Funding for Earth Sciences Scholarship Program for children of employees; giving focused primarily in corporate operating locations
$ Given: Of $1,200,000 coroporate giving total, 55–60% designated for education
Contact: Sonja B. Michaud, Foundation President

CORPORATE/EMPLOYEE PROGRAMS

American Brands, Inc.
1700 E. Putnam Avenue
P.O. Box 811
Old Greenwich, CT 06870
(203) 698–5148

Description: Support for wide range of educational programs; funding provided near headquarters and operating locations only
$ Given: $13,140,179 corporate giving total; amount to education not specified
Contact: Roger W.W. Baker, Secretary

CM Alliance Company
Connecticut Mutual Life Foundation
140 Garden Street
Hartford, CT 06154
(203) 727–6500

Description: Special consideration given to elementary and secondary schools in the Hartford area that stress employment skills and/or enhance opportunities for furthering education; matching gift program includes private secondary schools; special consideration to greater Hartford area and Connecticut
$ Given: Of $1,786,500 corporate giving total, 40–45% designated for education
Contact: Astrida R. Olds, Assistant Vice President

General Electric Company
GE Foundations
3135 Easton Turnpike
Fairfield, CT 06431
(203) 373–3216

Description: Three–fifths of education monies to colleges; one–sixth to federal associations and organizations; grants on pre–college level emphasize improvement of math and science teaching & criteria, and improvement of students' abilities in these areas; giving focused principally near corporate operations locations; national organizations also funded
$ Given: Of $39,000,000 corporate giving total, 50–55% designated for education
Contact: Clifford V. Smith, Jr., President

General Reinsurance Corporation
Financial Centre
P.O. Box 10350
Stanford, CT 06904
(203) 328–5000

Description: Funding for private secondary schools; giving focused near operating locations; national organizations also funded
$ Given: $1,300,000 corporate giving total; amount to education not specified
Contact: Richard K. Troxell, Assistant Vice President

GTE Corporation
GTE Foundation
One Stanford Forum
Stanford, CT 06904
(203) 965–3620

Description: Scholarships for secondary and undergraduate education; employee matching gifts program and scholarships for children of employees; funding for national programs; giving focused primarily in communities where company has business operations
$ Given: Of $20,407,202 corporate giving total, 50–55% designated for education
Contact: Maureen V. Gorman, Secretary

ITT Hartford Insurance Group
ITT Hartford Insurance Group Foundation
Hartford Plaza
690 Asylum Avenue
Hartford, CT 06115
(203) 547–4972

Description: Giving focused primarily in Hartford, Connecticut; requests from organizations in the 42 office communities around the country considered
$ Given: Of $3,000,000 corporate giving total, 25–30% designated for education
Contact: Sandra A. Sharr, Director of Community Affairs

Olin Corporation
Olin Corporation Charitable Trust
120 Long Ridge Road
Stanford, CT 06904
(203) 356–3301

Description: Support for private secondary schools through matching gifts; giving focused principally near operating locations; national organizations also funded
$ Given: Of $1,900,000 corporate giving total, 40–45% designated for education
Contact: Carmella V. Piacentini, Administrator

SNET
227 Church Street
New Haven, CT 06506
(203) 771–2546

Description: Funding only within the state of Connecticut
$ Given: Of $1,500,000 corporate giving total, 33% designated for education
Contact: Daisy Rodriguez, Manager, Corporate Relations

United Parcel Service of America
UPS Foundation
Greenwich Office Parks
Greenwich, CT 06831
(203) 862–6201

Description: Scholarships for children of employees; national funding provided
$ Given: Of $9,500,000 corporate giving total, 25–30% designated for education
Contact: Clem Hanrahan, Director

United Technologies Corporation
One Financial Plaza
Hartford, CT 06101
(203) 728–7943

Description: Three–quarters of education monies to colleges; matches employee gifts to colleges, universities and private secondary schools on a 1:1 basis; emphasis on communities where company operates
$ Given: Of $12,125,000 corporate giving total, 50–55% designated for education
Contact: Richard C. Cole, Director, Public Affairs

Xerox Corporation
Xerox Foundation
P.O. Box 1600
Stanford, CT 06904
(203) 968–3306

Description: National and international funding for private education, with emphasis on corporate operating locations
$ Given: Of $14,500,000 corporate giving total, 45–50% designated for education
Contact: Robert H. Gudger, Vice President

DELAWARE

Beneficial Corporation
Beneficial Foundation
P.O. Box 911
Wilmington, DE 19899
(302) 798–0800

Description: Scholarship support for children of Beneficial employees
$ Given: Of $600,000 corporate giving total, 65–70% designated for education
Contact: John O. Williams, Director

E.I. Du Pont De Nemours & Company
Du Pont Building, Rm. 8065
1007 Market Street
Wilmington, DE 19898
(302) 774–2036

Description: Secondary school grants emphasizing improvement of teaching in science and economics; giving focused near headquarters and operating locations; some national organizations also funded
$ Given: Of $28,000,000 corporate giving total, 50–55% designated for education
Contact: John T. Lund, Vice Chair & Executive Director of the Committee on Education Aid, (302) 774–5025

DISTRICT OF COLUMBIA

Giant Food
Giant Food Foundation
P.O. Box 1804, D–593
Washington, DC 20013
(202) 341–4301

Description: Funding provided in Maryland, Washington, DC and Virginia only
$ Given: Of $670,000 corporate giving total, 5% designated for education

Hitachi, Ltd.
Hitachi Foundation
1509 22nd Street, NW
Washington, DC 20037
(202) 457–0588

Description: Emphasis on projects that improve the quality of teaching and learning at all levels and show promise of enabling individuals to participate more fully in society; no geographic restrictions within the continental United States
$ Given: $2,000,000 corporate giving total; amount to education not specified
Contact: Felicia B. Lynch, Vice President, Programs

FLORIDA

Carnival Cruise Lines
Arison Foundation
One Centrust Financial Center
100 Southeast 2nd Street
Miami, FL 33131–2136
(305) 577–8200

Description: Funding provided primarily to organizations in the Miami area
$ Given: Of $1,089,688 corporate giving total, 5% designated for education
Contact: Shari Arison, President

Florida Power Corporation
P.O. Box 14042
St. Petersburg, FL 33733
(813) 866–5151

Description: Support for education and scholarship funds, and for private pre–college education; funding focused primarily in Florida, in Florida Power Corporation territories
$ Given: Of $750,000 corporate giving total, 50% designated for education
Contact: Maurice Phillips, Executive Vice President

Rinker Materials Corporation
Rinker Companies Foundation
1501 Belvedere Road
West Palm Beach, FL 33416
(305) 833–5555

Description: Funding for private secondary schools; giving focused primarily in Florida, with emphasis on Dade and Palm Beach counties
$ Given: Of $1,340,000 corporate giving total, 70–75% designated for education
Contact: Frank LaPlaca, Assistant Secretary

Winn–Dixie Stores
Winn–Dixie Stores Foundation
Box B
Jacksonville, FL 32203
(904) 783–5000

Description: Giving focused primarily in the company's 13–state trade area, generally within the Southeastern United States
$ Given: $1,800,000 corporate giving total; amount to education not specified
Contact: Larry H. May, President

GEORGIA

Citizens & Southern Corporation
Citizens & Southern Fund
P.O. Box 4899
Atlanta, GA 30302
(404) 581–2496

Description: Support limited to those areas where service is provided by company, primarily in the state of Georgia
$ Given: Of $1,800,000 corporate giving total, 25–30% designated for education
Contact: Kirby A. Thompson, Secretary & Treasurer

CORPORATE/EMPLOYEE PROGRAMS

Coca–Cola Company
Coca–Cola Foundation
P.O. Drawer 1734
Atlanta, GA 30301
(404) 676–2680

Description: Employee matching gifts programs; special consideration to organizations located in Atlanta and to organizations in other major bases of operation (Houston, New York, Los Angeles)
$ Given: Of $5,138,530 annual corporate giving total, 25–30% designated for education; Coca–Cola has also allocated $50 million ($5 million per year) to be used solely for the purpose of supporting education
Contact: Donald R. Greene, President

First Atlanta Corporation
First Atlanta Foundation
First National Bank
of Atlanta
P.O. Box 4148, MC: 1530
Atlanta, GA 30302
(404) 332–6592

Description: Funding provided in operating locations only
$ Given: Of $900,000 corporate giving total, 20–25% designated for education

Georgia Power Company
Georgia Power Foundation
333 Piedmont Avenue
20th Floor
Atlanta, GA 30308
(404) 526–6784

Description: Funding in Georgia, with emphasis on Atlanta
$ Given: Of $3,323,196 corporate giving total, 25–30% designated for education
Contact: Judy Andersen, Executive Director

J.P. Stevens & Company
West Point–Pepperell
Foundation
P.O. Box 342
West 10th Street
West Point, GA 31833
(404) 645–4879

Description: Support for private pre–college education; funding focused in communities where J.P. Stevens maintains operating facilities
$ Given: Of $1,253,317 corporate giving total, 65–70% designated for education
Contact: Toni Cauble

Trust Company Bank
Trust Company of Georgia
Foundation
Mail Code 041
P.O. Box 4418
Atlanta, GA 30302
(404) 588–8246

Description: Over one–half of education monies to colleges and universities; private schools also major recipients; funding in metropolitan Atlanta (Fulton and Dekalb counties) only
$ Given: Of $1,430,000 corporate giving total, 40–45% designated for education
Contact: Victor A. Gregory, Secretary

HAWAII

AMFAC/JMB Hawaii, Inc.
P.O. Box 3230
Honolulu, HI 96801
(808) 945–8111

Description: Emphasis on student aid, colleges & universities, private education; grants made exclusively in Hawaii
$ Given: Of $566,000 corporate giving total, 15% designated for education
Contact: Linda Rosehill, Public Affairs Manager

HEI Inc.
Hawaiian Electric Industries Charitable Foundation
900 Richands Street
Honolulu, HI 96813
(808) 543–7333

Description: Support for secondary and higher education; funding primarily in Hawaii
$ Given: Of $1,000,000 corporate giving total, 15–20% designated for education
Contact: George T. Iwahiro, Vice President and Director

IDAHO

Boise Cascade Corporation
One Jefferson Square
P.O. Box 50
Boise, ID 83728–0001
(208) 384–7673

Description: Match program for employees' gifts to secondary schools; giving focused near operating locations; national organizations also funded
$ Given: Of $2,200,000 corporate giving total, 30–35% designated for education
Contact: Connie E. Weaver, Contributions Administrator

ILLINOIS

Abbott Laboratories
Abbott Laboratories Fund
One Abbott Park Road
D379 Building AP14C
Abbott Park, IL 60064–3500
(708) 937–8686 or 937–7075

Description: Grants given for private higher and secondary education
$ Given: Of total corporate employee grant monies, 40% designated for education
Contact: Cindy Schwab, Administrator

AON Corporation
AON Foundation
123 N. Wacker Drive
Chicago, IL 60606
(312) 701–3035

Description: Major support to Northwestern University; support for pre–college private education; giving focused primarily in operating locations
$ Given: Of $2,041,456 corporate giving total, 25–30% designated for education
Contact: Wallace J. Buya, Vice President & Corporation Secretary

CORPORATE/EMPLOYEE PROGRAMS

Borg–Warner Corporation
Borg–Warner Foundation
200 South Michigan Avenue
Chicago, IL 60604
(312) 322–8659

Description: Funding primarily in Chicago
$ Given: Of $1,500,000 corporate giving total, 45–50% designated for education
Contact: Ellen J. Benjamin, Director, Corporate Contributions

CLARCOR
CLARCOR Foundation
P.O. Box 7007
Rockford, IL 61125
(815) 962–8861

Description: Two–thirds of educational grant monies given to colleges and universities; emphasis on operating locations, especially Rockford, Illinois
$ Given: Of $500,000 corporate giving total, 50–55% designated for education
Contact: William Knese, Chair

Deere & Company
John Deere Foundation
John Deere Road
Moline, IL 61265
(309) 765–5030

Description: Support for pre–college, private education in areas where Deere and Company maintains facilities; some national organizations also funded
$ Given: Of $4,391,440 corporate giving total, 15% designated for education
Contact: Donald R. Margenthaler, President

R.R. Donnelly & Sons Company
2223 Martin Luther King Dr.
Chicago, IL 60616
(312) 326–8102

Description: Support for college and pre–college private education; matching program for employee gifts to higher and secondary education; scholarships for children of employees; funding focused primarily near operating locations; national organizations also funded
$ Given: Of $2,800,000 corporate giving total, 25–35% designated for education
Contact: Susan Levy, Community Relations Manager

Duchossois Industries
Duchossois Industries Foundation
845 Larch Avenue
Elmhurst, IL 60126
(312) 279–3600

Description: Limited support to higher education and youth programs; funding primarily in Chicago
$ Given: Of $450,000 corporate giving total, 15–20% designated for education
Contact: Kimberly D. Lenczuk, Secretary

• • • • • • • • • • • • • • • • • • •

GATX Corporation
120 S. Riverside Plaza
Chicago, IL 60606
(312) 621-6221

Description: Matching programs for employee gifts to schools; funding focused primarily in Chicago and in other locations where company does business
$ Given: $1,200,000 corporate giving total
Contact: Christiane S. Wilczure, Manager, Community Affairs

Hartmarx Corporation
Hartmarx Charitable Foundation
101 N. Wacker Drive
Chicago, IL 60606
(312) 372-6300

Description: Funding provided near headquarters and operating locations only
$ Given: Of $850,000 corporate giving total, 20% designated for education
Contact: Kay Nolbach, President

IMCERA Group, Inc.
IMCERA Foundation
2315 Sanders Road
Northbrook, IL 60062
(708) 564-8600

Description: Project support at the primary and secondary levels; funding focused primarily in Chicago and other operating locations in the Midwest
$ Given: Of $1,400,000 corporate giving total, 10–15% designated for education
Contact: Colleen D. Keast, Manager, Public Affairs

Interlake Corporation
Interlake Foundation
701 Harger Road
Oak Brook, IL 60521
(708) 572-6600

Description: Scholarships for children of employees sponsored through the National Merit Scholarship Corporation; funding focused primarily in the Chicago metropolitian area; various operating locations also funded
$ Given: Of $370,000 corporate giving total, 35–40% designated for education
Contact: David Downs, Vice President, Human Resources

Kraft General Foods
Kraft General Foods Foundation
Kraft Court 2W
Glenview, IL 60025
(312) 998-7032

Description: Focus on structural changes in grades K through 12 and on strengthening of education, health & nutrition, and culture & humanities; primarily concerned with programs and organizations that have national impact or that benefit communities where company employees live and work
$ Given: Of $11,977,294 corporate giving total, 40% designated for education
Contact: Ronald J. Coman, Administrative Director

CORPORATE/EMPLOYEE PROGRAMS

Montgomery Ward & Company
Montgomery Ward Foundation
One Montgomery Ward Plaza, 8–A
Chicago, IL 60671
(312) 467–7663

Description: Support for educational institutions and organizations provided almost entirely through an employee matching gift program; major emphasis on corporate headquarters in Chicago
$ Given: Of $813,000 corporate giving total, 20% designated for education
Contact: Charles Holland, Secretary

Motorola
Motorola Foundation
1303 E. Algonquin Road
Schaumburg, IL 60196
(708) 576–6200

Description: Nearly all gifts in the form of direct grants to colleges & universities, and matching gifts to colleges, universities & private secondary schools; funding focused primarily near headquarters and major plant locations
$ Given: Of $3,500,000 corporate giving total, 55–60% designated for education
Contact: Herta Betty Nikola, Administrator

Nalco Chemical Company
Nalco Chemical Foundation
One Nalco Center
Naperville, IL 60563–1198
(708) 305–1556

Description: Funding for private, pre–college education and student aid; restricted to towns where Nalco has major manufacturing facilities or subsidiaries; emphasis on Chicago metropolitan area, including Du Page County
$ Given: Of $1,700,000 corporate giving total, 35% designated for education
Contact: Joanne C. Ford, President

Quaker Oats Company
Quaker Oats Foundation
321 N. Clark Street
Suite 13–3
Chicago, IL 60610
(312) 222–7377

Description: Much of support provided through employee matching gifts; giving focused principally near operating locations; national organizations also funded
$ Given: Of $2,765,000 corporate giving total, 40–42% designated for education
Contact: Charles E. Curry, Assistant Secretary

USG Corporation
USG Foundation
101 S. Wacker Drive
Chicago, IL 60606
(312) 606–4000

Description: National support to private preparatory schools, with emphasis on Illinois and corporate operating locations
$ Given: Of $400,000 corporate giving total, 35–40% designated for education
Contact: Eugene Miller, President

INDIANA

Arvin Industries
Arvin Foundation
One Noblitt Plaza
Box 3000
Columbus, IN 47202–3000
(812) 379–3285

Description: Grant monies given for student aid; funding provided principally near operating locations, especially in Indiana, and to some state and national organizations
$ Given: Of $623,542 corporate giving total, 45–55% designated for education
Contact: J. William Kendall, Chair, Gifts Committee

Cummins Engine Company
Cummins Engine Foundation
Box 3005
Mail Code 60814
Columbus, IN 47202
(812) 377–3114

Description: Emphasis on improving elementary and secondary schools; funding provided primarily in communities where Cummins Engine Company has manufacturing operations
$ Given: Of $4,000,000 corporate giving total, 30–40% designated for education

IOWA

Rolscreen Company
Pella Rolscreen Foundation
102 Main Street
Pella, IA 50219
(515) 628–1000

Description: Support for private pre–college education; scholarship program for children of company employees
$ Given: Of $1,000,000 corporate giving total, 45–50% designated for education
Contact: William J. Anderson, Administrator

KANSAS

United Telecommunications Inc.
United Telecommunications Inc. Foundation
2330 Shawnee Mission Pkwy
Westwood, KS 66205
(816) 276–6940

Description: Funding provided primarily in the Kansas City area and near corporate and subsidiary operating locations
$ Given: $1,675,000 corporate giving total; amount to education not specified
Contact: Don Forsythe, Vice President

KENTUCKY

Ashland Oil
Ashland Oil Foundation
P.O. Box 391
Ashland, KY
(606) 329–4525

Description: Employee matching gifts program to educational institutions; giving focused near corporate facilities, primarily in Appalachia
$ Given: Of $4,000,000 corporate giving total, 55–60% designated for education
Contact: Judy B. Thomas, President

Citizens Fidelity Bank & Trust Co.
Citizens Fidelity Foundation
Citizens Plaza
Louisville, KY 40296
(502) 581–2811

Description: Support for private pre–college education; funding provided near headquarters and operating locations only
$ Given: Grants range from $1,000 to $10,000; of $1,000,000 corporate giving total, 20–25% designated for education
Contact: Jessica Loving, Vice President, Corporate Affairs

Humana
Humana Foundation
500 W. Main Street
P.O. Box 1438
Louisville, KY 40201
(502) 580–3920

Description: Support for public and private pre–college education; funding provided in company business areas, with emphasis on Louisville, Kentucky
$ Given: Of $6,156,512 corporate giving total, 45–50% designated for education
Contact: Joy Foley, Contributions Manager

LOUISIANA

Louisiana Land & Exploration Company
Louisiana Land & Exploration Foundation
P.O. Box 60350
New Orleans, LA 70160
(504) 566–6500

Description: One–third of education funds in the form of employee matching gifts; scholarship program for children of employees; funding focused in company operating locations
$ Given: Grants range from $1,000 to $10,000; of $675,000 corporate giving total, 50–55% designated for education
Contact: Karen A. Overson

MARYLAND

First Maryland Bank Corp.
First Maryland Foundation
25 S. Charles Street
Baltimore, MD 21201
(301) 244–4907

Description: Monies given for student aid; emphasis on greater Baltimore and the state of Maryland
$ Given: Of $1,170,000 corporate giving total, 35–40% designated for education
Contact: Robert W. Schaefer, Secretary–Treasurer & Trustee

Hechinger Company
Hechinger Foundation
1616 McCormick Drive
Landover, MD 20785
(301) 341–0999

Description: Funding focused near headquarters and operating locations
$ Given: Of $1,200,000 corporate giving total, 15–20% designated for education
Contact: Richard England, President

MNC Financial
MNC Financial Foundation
P.O. Box 987–MS250332
Baltimore, MD 21203
(301) 547–4126

Description: Funding for private and public schools' construction and program costs; support for innovative educational programs; funding focused in Maryland
$ Given: Of $3,600,000 corporate giving total, 30% designated for education
Contact: George B.P. Ward, Jr., Secretary & Treasurer

Noxell Corporation
Noxell Foundation
11050 York Road
Hunt Valley, MD 21030
(301) 785–4313

Description: Some emphasis on private schools; emphasis on Baltimore metropolitan area; some support to national organizations
$ Given: Of $1,600,000 corporate giving total, 25–30% designated for education
Contact: William R. McCartin, Treasurer

Signet Bank/Maryland
Signet Bank/Maryland Charitable Trust
P.O. Box 1077–T0307
Baltimore, MD 21203
(301) 332–5194

Description: Funding provided in Baltimore metropolitan area and on Maryland's Eastern Shore
$ Given: $646,000 corporate giving total; amount to education not specified
Contact: Patricia K. Sisley, Vice President, Public Affairs

USF&G Company
USF&G Company
Foundation
100 Light Street
Baltimore, MD 21202
(301) 547-3310

Description: Scholarships to children of employees; limited support to education funds and private secondary schools; giving provided primarily in operating locations and to national organizations
$ Given: Of $4,470,000 corporate giving total, 25–30% designated for education
Contact: William Spliedt, Secretary & Treasurer

MASSACHUSETTS

Cabot Corporation
Cabot Corporation
Foundation
950 Winter Street
Waltham, MA 02154
(617) 890-0200

Description: Support for secondary school science and mathematics education, particularly programs focused on gifted students; matching gifts account for one-third of funding; giving focused principally near operating locations
$ Given: Grants range from $2,500 to $15,000; of $950,000 corporate giving total, 55–60% designated for education
Contact: Dorothy L. Forbes, Executive Director; or manager of local Cabot facility

FMR Corporation
Fidelity Foundation
82 Devonshire Street
Boston, MA 02109
(617) 570-6806

Description: Employee matching gifts program; accepts proposals from organizations located in greater Boston area and in regions recommended by Fidelity managers
$ Given: $2,000,000 corporate giving total; amount to education not specified
Contact: Anne-Marie Soulliere, Foundation Director

Norton Company
Norton Company
Foundation
120 Front Street
Worcester, MA 01608
(508) 795-5773

Description: Support for secondary education; matching gifts program; giving focused in communities where Norton Company maintains facilities
$ Given: Of $1,100,000 corporate giving total, 25–30% designated for education
Contact: Francis J. Doherty, Jr.

Polaroid Corporation
Polaroid Foundation
750 Main Street
2nd Floor
Cambridge, MA 02139
(617) 577-3470

Description: Support for private elementary and secondary education; matching gifts and scholarships for children of employees; giving focused primarily in greater Boston/Cambridge area
$ Given: Of $2,100,000 corporate giving total, 20–25% designated for education
Contact: Marcia Schiff, Executive Director

Stop and Shop Companies Inc.
Stop and Shop Charitable Foundation
P.O. Box 369
Boston, MA 02101
(617) 770–8000

Description: Funding for private pre–college education, primarily in Massachusetts and other operating locations
$ Given: Of $659,895 corporate giving total, 20–25% designated for education
Contact: Missy Grealy, Director of Corporate Affairs

MICHIGAN

Chrysler Corporation
Chrysler Corporation Fund
12000 Chrysler Drive
Highland Park, MI
48288–1919
(313) 956–5194

Description: Approximately one-half of educational support to pre–college education programs and institutions; one–twelfth of support in matching gifts to private secondary schools; scholarships awarded to children of employees; funding provided near operating locations and to national organizations
$ Given: Of $11,700,000 corporate giving total, 45–50% designated for education

Gerber Companies Foundation
445 State Street
Freemont, MI 49412
(616) 928–2759

Description: Scholarships to employee families;; areas of support include pre–school education, special education and student aid
$ Given: Grants range from $100 to $3,000; 33% of corporate giving total designated for education
Contact: John B. Whitlock, Administrator

NBD Bank
NBD Charitable Trust
P.O. Box 222
Detroit, MI 48232
(313) 225–3735

Description: Emphasis on Detroit, Michigan
$ Given: Of $2,800,000 corporate giving total, 20% designated for education
Contact: Sharon Maye, Manager, Contributions & Memberships

Steelcase
Steelcase Foundation
P.O. Box 1967
Grand Rapids, MI 49501
(616) 246–4695

Description: Funding for private education, provided exclusively in areas where company has manufacturing operations
$ Given: Of $3,143,358 corporate giving total, 20% designated for education
Contact: Kate Pew Wolters, Executive Director

Whirlpool Corporation
Whirlpool Foundation
2000 M63
Benton Harbor, MI 49022
(616) 926–3461

Description: Funding provided in areas where Whirlpool maintains manufacturing facilities
$ Given: Of $3,600,000 corporate giving total, 30–35% designated for education
Contact: Sharron Krieger, Executive Director & Secretary

MINNESOTA

Andersen Corporation
Bayport Foundation
100 Fourth Avenue North
Bayport, MN 55003–1096
(612) 439–5150

Description: Grant monies given for student aid; funding provided predominantly in Minnesota, especially Twin Cities area; funding also given in St. Croix, Wisconsin area, and to national organizations
$ Given: Of $700,000 corporate giving total, 12% designated for education
Contact: W. Arvid Wellman, President

Bemis Company
Bemis Company Foundation
625 Marquette Avenue
Minneapolis, MN 55402
(612) 340–6198

Description: Approximately one–third of support through educational matching gifts and scholarship programs for children of employees; funding provided in areas where company maintains facilities, with emphasis on Minneapolis, Minnesota
$ Given: Of $714,542 corporate giving total, 40–45% designated for education
Contact: Lawrence E. Schwanke, Trustee

Cargill, Inc.
Cargill Foundation
P.O. Box 9300
Minneapolis, MN 55440
(612) 475–6213

Description: Scholarships awarded almost exclusively in Minneapolis/St. Paul area
$ Given: Of $5,000,000 corporate giving total, 35–40% designated for education
Contact: Audrey R. Tulberg, Program and Administration Director, (612) 475–6122; or contact nearest Cargill office directly

Cowles Media Company
Cowles Media Foundation
329 Portland Avenue
Minneapolis, MN 55415
(612) 673–7051

Description: Funding provided near headquarters and operating locations only
$ Given: Of $1,700,000 corporate giving total, 20% designated for education
Contact: Jan Schwichtenberg, Contributions Coordinator

First Bank System
First Bank System Foundation
P.O. Box 522, MPFW0105
Minneapolis, MN 55480
(612) 370–5176

Description: Matching program for employee gifts to education; interest in grades K through 12 education reform
$ Given: Of $5,145,000 corporate giving total, 15–25% designated for education
Contact: Barbara B. Roy, Executive Director

H.B. Fuller Company
H.B. Fuller Company Foundation
2400 Energy Park Drive
St. Paul, MN 55108
(612) 647–3617

Description: National funding, with emphasis on headquarter and operating communities
$ Given: Of $200,000 corporate giving total, 20–25% designated for education
Contact: Karen P. Muller, Executive Director

General Mills
General Mills Foundation
P.O. Box 1113
Minneapolis, MN 55440
(612) 540–7890

Description: One–half of education monies given to higher education; additional support for pre–college education; about one–fourth of educational giving through employee matching gifts program; funding provided primarily in communities where the company has a substantial number of employees
$ Given: Of $10,500,000 corporate giving total, 20–25% designated for education
Contact: Reatha Clark King, President & Executive Director

Graco
Graco Foundation
P.O. Box 1441
Minneapolis, MN 55440–1441
(612) 623–6684

Description: Scholarships for children of employees; focus on the state of Minnesota, particularly Minneapolis, where foundation places special emphasis on grants serving the Northeast and near north neighborhoods; limited support to other communities where company has a significant number of employees
$ Given: Of $860,000 corporate giving total, 30–35% designated for education
Contact: Elizabeth M. Jaros, Executive Director

IDS Financial Services
American Express Minnesota Foundation
2100 IDS Tower
Minneapolis, MN 55440
(612) 372–3321

Description: Giving focused primarily in the Twin Cities, with some giving in greater Minnesota
$ Given: Of $2,500,000 corporate giving total, 20% designated for education
Contact: Marie L. Tobin, Community Relations Specialist

• • • • • • • • • • • • • • • • • • •

Jostens
Jostens Foundation, Inc.
5501 Norman Center Drive
Minneapolis, MN 55437
(612) 830–8429

Description: Major support to scholarship program for children of employees; giving focused primarily in Minneapolis and St. Paul
$ Given: Of $1,938,398 corporate giving total, 40–45% designated for education
Contact: Ellis F. Bullock, Jr., Executive Director

Medtronic
Medtronic Foundation
7000 Central Avenue, NE
Minneapolis, MN 55432
(612) 574–3024

Description: Employee matching gifts program; funding to elementary and secondary education; giving focused in Medtronic plant communities, with emphasis on Minneappolis/St. Paul area
$ Given: Of $1,724,000 corporate giving total, 20–25% designated for education
Contact: Jan Schwarz, Manager

Norwest Corporation
Norwest Foundation
Norwest Center
Sixth & Marquette
Minneapolis, MN
55479–1055
(612) 667–7860

Description: Support of private institutions generally channeled through education funds; funding provided in upper Midwestern states: Iowa, Minnesota, Montana, North Dakota, Nebraska, South Dakota and Wisconsin
$ Given: Of $5,600,000 corporate giving total, 25–30% designated for education
Contact: Diane P. Lilly, President

Saint Paul Companies
385 Washington Street
St. Paul, MN 55102
(612) 221–7875

Description: Support for private college and pre–college education; scholarships for children of employees; giving focused primarily in St. Paul, Minnesota
$ Given: Of $5,500,000 corporate giving total, 25% designated for education
Contact: Polly Nyberg, Community Affairs Manager

MISSOURI

H & R Block
H & R Block Foundation
4410 Main Street
Kansas City, MO 64111
(816) 753–6900

Description: Scholarship grants to children of employees; private secondary schools eligible for matching gifts; funding provided near headquarters and operating locations only
$ Given: Of $1,020,751 corporate giving total, 30–40% designated for education
Contact: Terrence R. Ward, President

CPI Corporation
CPI Philanthropic Trust
1706 Washington Avenue
St. Louis, MO 63103
(314) 231-1575

Description: Support for private pre-college education; almost all grants awarded in Missouri
$ Given: Grants range from $500 to $5,000; of $819,000 corporate giving total, 25-30% designated for education
Contact: Fran Scheper

Emerson Electric Company
Emerson Charitable Trust
P.O. Box 4100
8000 W. Florissant Avenue
St. Louis, MO 63136
(314) 553-3722

Description: Employee matching grants program in education; educational scholarship program for children of employees; funding provided nationally, with emphasis on company operating communities
$ Given: Of $9,105,000 corporate giving total, 30-35% designated for education
Contact: Jo Anne Hermon, Vice President, Corporate Administration

Laclede Gas Company
Laclede Gas
Charitable Trust
720 Olive Street, Rm. 63101
St. Louis, MO 63101
(314) 342-0506

Description: Student aid and employee matching gift programs; funding provided almost exclusively in Missouri, principally in company's service area, St. Louis
$ Given: Of $502,730 corporate giving total, 20-25% designated for education
Contact: David L. Gardner, Trustee

Mercantile Bank Corp.
Mercantile Trust Co.
Charitable Trust
Mercantile Tower
P.O. Box 387
St. Louis, MO 63166
(314) 425-2610

Description: Funding provided near headquarters and operating locations only
$ Given: Of $1,200,000 corporate giving total, 15-20% designated for education
Contact: Walter F. Gray, Executive Vice President

Monsanto Company
Monsanto Fund
800 N. Lindbergh Boulevard
St. Louis, MO 63167
(314) 694-4596

Description: Support for both pre-college and higher education institutions with strong emphasis on science, engineering, agriculture, and chemistry; giving focused primarily where Monsanto has operating facilities; select national organizations also funded
$ Given: Of $13,600,000 corporate giving total, 40% designated for education
Contact: John L. Mason, President

Pulitzer Publishing Company
Pulitzer Publishing Foundation
900 N. Tucker Boulevard
St. Louis, MO 63101
(314) 622-7357

Description: Funding for private pre-college education, primarily in St. Louis metropolitan area
$ Given: Of $500,000 corporate giving total, 20-25% designated for education
Contact: Ronald H. Ridgway, Treasurer & Director

Ralston Purina Company
Ralston Purina Trust Fund
Checkerboard Square
St. Louis, MO 63164
(314) 982-3234

Description: Four-fifths of education monies to universities; additional support for private pre-college education; giving focused primarily in St. Louis and company plant locations
$ Given: Of $2,514,416 corporate giving total, 35-40% designated for education
Contact: Fred H. Perabo, Secretary, Board of Control

Union Electric Company
Union Electric Company Charitable Trust
P.O. Box 149
St. Louis, MO 63166
(314) 554-2521

Description: Funding provided near headquarters and operating locations only
$ Given: Of $2,000,000 corporate giving total, 30-35% designated for education
Contact: Patricia Barrett, Manager, Community Services

Wetterau Inc.
8920 Pershall Road
Hazelwood, MO 63042
(314) 524-5000

Description: Support for programs designed to improve education at various levels, with an emphasis on primary and secondary schools; funding provided near headquarters and operating locations only
$ Given: $752,487 corporate giving total; amount to education not specified, but education is a high priority
Contact: Joyce Pinkowski, Contributions Coordinator

NEBRASKA

Con Agra
Con Agra Charitable Foundation
One Central Park Plaza
Omaha, NE 68102
(402) 978-4160

Description: Four-fifths of education monies given to colleges; one-tenth to business education; funding focused primarily in Nebraska, particularly in Omaha
$ Given: Of $1,087,909 corporate giving total, 20-25% designated for education
Contact: Martin G. Colladay, Vice President & Foundation Manager

Peter Kiewit Sons
Peter Kiewit Sons
Foundation
1000 Kiewit Plaza
Omaha, NE 68131
(402) 342–2052

Description: Funding focused principally in Omaha and in locations where company has significant operations
$ Given: Of $1,800,000 corporate giving total, 20% designated for education
Contact: Mike Faust, Assistant to Chair

Omaha World Herald Company
Omaha World Herald
Company Foundation
14th & Dodge Streets
Omaha, NE 68102
(402) 444–1413

Description: Half of education monies support Nebraska College; grants also support public and private pre–college education; funding provided primarily in Omaha, Nebraska, and to regional organizations and institutions
$ Given: Of $850,000 corporate giving total, 35–40% designated for education
Contact: Terry Ausenbaugh, Administration Manager

NEW JERSEY

Allied Signal
Allied Signal Foundation
P.O. Box 2245R
Morristown, NJ 07962
(201) 455–5876

Description: Grants made near operating locations and to national organizations
$ Given: Of $10,000,000 corporate giving total, 45–50% designated for education
Contact: Alan S. Painter, Vice President & Executive Director

Campbell Soup Company
Campbell Soup Fund
Campbell Place
Camden, NJ 08101–1799
(609) 342–6424

Description: Funding provided near company headquarters and operating facilities in United States only
$ Given: Of $1,600,000 corporate giving total, 30% designated for education
Contact: Jeremiah F. O'Brien, Fund Vice Chair

CPC International, Inc.
International Plaza
P.O. Box 8000
Englewood Cliffs, NJ 07632
(201) 894–2521

Description: Funding provided primarily near operating locations and to national organizations
$ Given: Of $650,000 corporate giving total, 40–45% designated for education
Contact: Patricia Biale, Manager, Personnel Services

CORPORATE/EMPLOYEE PROGRAMS

Crum & Forster, Inc.
Crum & Forster Foundation
211 Mt. Airy Road
Basking Ridge, NJ 07920
(201) 204-3540

Description: Education monies given to private secondary school education; funding provided principally near headquarters and operating locations, and to national organizations
$ Given: Of $1,012,000 corporate giving total, 25% designated for education
Contact: Ruth Goodell, Corporate Contributions Administrator

Mutual Benefit Life Insurance Co.
Mutual Benefit Life Charitable Trust
520 Broad St., Rm. AO5N
Newark, NJ 07101
(201) 481-8113

Description: Highest priority objective: to improve educational systems and quality of education in home office cities, giving company a source of capable potential employees; funding focused principally in Newark, New Jersey and Kansas City, Missouri
$ Given: $2,117,550 corporate giving total; amount to education not specified
Contact: Florence Demming, Public Affairs Manager

National Westminister Bank, NJ
10 Exchange Place Center
Jersey City, NJ 07302
(201) 547-7000

Description: Funding provided near headquarters and operating locations only
$ Given: $750,000 corporate giving total; amount to education not specified
Contact: Robert W. Call, Senior Vice President

Prudential Insurance Co. of America
Prudential Foundation
Prudential Plaza
751 Broad Street, 15th Floor
Newark, NJ 07102-3777
(201) 802-7354

Description: Employee matching gifts program for private secondary schools; funding focused near operating locations with special emphasis on New Jersey and the city of Newark
$ Given: Of $15,524,000 corporate giving total, 30–35% designated for education
Contact: Elisa D. Puzzuoli, Secretary

Public Service Electric & Gas Company
80 Park Plaza
P.O. Box 570
Newark, NJ 07101
(201) 430-5763

Description: Support for pre–college education; scholarships; match program for employee gifts to institutions; funding provided primarily in service area; education grants awarded nationally
$ Given: $2,600,000 corporate giving total; amount to education not specified
Contact: Oswald L. Cano, General Manager, Corporate Responsibility

Union Camp Corporation
Union Camp
Charitable Trust
1600 Valley Road
Wayne, NJ 07470
(201) 628–2248

Description: Funding provided principally near operating locations and to national organizations
$ Given: Of $3,000,000 corporate giving total, 40–45% designated for education
Contact: Sydney N. Phin, H.R. Director

NEW YORK

American Express Company
American Express Foundation
American Express Tower
World Financial Center
New York, NY 10285–4710
(212) 640–5661

Description: Employee matching gifts for education/culture; scholarships to children of employees
Contact: Cornelia W. Higginson, Vice President, International Philanthropic Program; Mary Beth Salerno, Vice President, Domestic Philanthropic Program

Bank of New York
48 Wall Street, 10th Floor
New York, NY 10286
(212) 495–1730

Description: Largely restricted to company operating areas in New York State
$ Given: $2,600,000 corporate giving total; amount to education not specified
Contact: Katherine C. Hastings, Assistant Vice President

Bausch & Lomb
Bausch & Lomb
Foundation
One Lincoln First Square
Rochester, NY 14601
(716) 338–5174

Description: Scholarships awarded principally in Rochester, New York
$ Given: Of $1,650,000 corporate giving total, 30–35% designated for education
Contact: Debra Buckett, Senior Administrator, Public Affairs

Capital Cities/ABC
Capital Cities Foundation
77 West 66th Street
16th Floor
New York, NY 10023
(212) 456–7011

Description: Funding provided near headquarters and operating locations only
$ Given: Of $2,000,000 corporate giving total, 40–45% designated for education
Contact: Bernadette Williams, Contributions Administrator

CORPORATE/EMPLOYEE PROGRAMS

• • • • • • • • • • • • • • • • • • •

Chase Manhattan Bank
Chase Manhattan
Foundation
2 Chase Plaza, 29th Floor
New York, NY 10081
(212) 552–9127

Description: Scholarships for children of employees; funding focused primarily near headquarters and operating locations; funding also given nationally
$ Given: Of $11,814,000 corporate giving total, 20% designated for education
Contact: David S. Ford, Vice President & Director of Philanthropy

Citicorp/Citibank
399 Park Avenue
New York, NY 10043
(212) 559–8182

Description: Program that matches employee gifts to education; funding provided in New York City and near operating locations nationwide
$ Given: Of $23,000,000 corporate giving total, 55–60% designated for education
Contact: Donna Stiansen, Manager, Corporate Contributions

First Boston
First Boston
Foundation Trust
12 East 49th Street
New York, NY 10017
(212) 909–4571

Description: Grants supporting economic and minority education, general programs and pre–college private education; funding provided nationally and near operating locations
$ Given: Of $1,500,000 corporate giving total, 50% designated for education
Contact: Maria Lilly, Director, Corporate Contributions

Forbes
Forbes Foundation
60 Fifth Avenue
New York, NY 10011
(212) 620–2248

Description: Funding provided primarily to colleges and universities in New York City area
$ Given: Of $1,489,126 corporate giving total, 15–20% designated for education
Contact: Leonard H. Yablon, President

IBM Corporation
2000 Purchase Street
Purchase, NY 10577
(914) 697–7617

Description: In 1990, IBM donated $4.4 million worth of computers and software to three elementary schools in Austin, Texas, participating in IBM's Project A+, a five–year, $25 million progam of cash and equipment grants to improve teacher preparation for use of computers and to stimulate new uses for computers in the classroom in elementary and secondary schools nationwide; funding provided nationally in areas of company facilities
$ Given: Of $135,000,000 corporate giving total, 40–45% designated for education
Contact: A.N. Scallon, Director

International Paper Company
International Paper Company Foundation
Two Manhattan Road
Purchase, NY 10577
(914) 397–1581

Description: Focus on improving the quality of pre-college teaching and learning in operating communities; funding provided primarily in communities where company facilities are located
$ Given: Of $2,500,000 corporate giving total, 25–30% designated for education
Contact: Sandra C. Wilson, Vice President; mill or plant managers, communications managers, human resources managers, or public affairs managers

Johnson and Higgins
125 Broad Street
New York, NY 10004
(212) 574–7028

Description: No geographic restrictions
$ Given: Of $2,400,000 corporate giving total, 33% designated for education
Contact: Frederick H. Kingsbury III

Kidder, Peabody & Company
Kidder Peabody Foundation
20 Exchange Place
New York, NY 10005
(212) 510–5502

Description: Funding provided principally near headquarters and operating locations
$ Given: Of $1,500,000 corporate giving total, 65–70% designated for education
Contact: Helen Platt, President

MacAndrews & Forbes Holdings
MacAndrews & Forbes Foundation
767 Fifth Avenue
New York, NY 10153
(212) 572–5980

Description: Seven–eighths of education monies given to the University of Pennsylvania, with the remainder given to private pre–college schools, legal & medical education, and Jewish studies; funding focused primarily in New York City
$ Given: Of $723,602 corporate giving total, 5–10% designated for education
Contact: James Conroy, Vice President, Corporate Affairs

R.H. Macy and Company
151 W. 34th Street
New York, NY 10001
(212) 560–4312

Description: Funding provided in company operating locations
$ Given: Of $3,000,000 corporate giving total, 10–15% designated for education
Contact: G.G. Michelson, Senior Vice President, External Affairs

Marsh & McLennan Companies
1166 Avenue of the Americas
New York, NY 10036
(212) 345–5645

Description: Funding provided to national and regional organizations
$ Given: $4,300,000 corporate giving total; amount to education not specified
Contact: Gloria Chin, Contributions Administrator

Milliken & Company
Milliken Foundation
1045 Avenue of the Americas
New York, NY 10018
(803) 573–2904

Description: Funding provided nationally and near operating locations
$ Given: Of $1,150,000 corporate giving total, 35–40% designated for education
Contact: Lawrence Heagney, Secretary

Morgan Guaranty Trust Company of New York
Morgan Guaranty Trust Company of New York Charitable Trust
60 Wall Street
New York, NY 10260
(212) 648–9673

Description: Two–fifths of education grants as matching gifts
$ Given: Of $10,047,207 corporate giving total, 25–30% designated for education
Contact: Robert A. Ruocco, Vice President, Community Relations & Public Affairs

New York Times Company
New York Times Company Foundation
229 W. 43rd Street
New York, NY 10036
(212) 556–1091

Description: Particularly interested in minority education, arts and journalism programs and scholarships, and in pre–college education; one–third of education monies awarded to match employee contributions to higher, secondary or elementary education; concentration on New York area and localities served by affiliates of company
$ Given: Of $5,228,268 corporate giving total, 30% designated for education
Contact: Fred M. Hechinger, President

Paramount Communications, Inc.
Paramount Communications Foundation
15 Columbus Circle
New York, NY 10023
(212) 373–8517

Description: Funding provided primarily in corporate operating locations
$ Given: $2,300,000 corporate giving total; amount to education not specified

Pfizer Inc.
Pfizer Foundation
235 E. 42nd Street
New York, NY 10017–5755
(212) 573–7578

Description: Funding for private education nationally and in communities where Pfizer and its subsidiaries operate; some emphasis on New York City
$ Given: Of $10,000,000 corporate giving total, 20% designated for education
Contact: Ann M. Hardwick, Manager, Corporate Support Programs

Quantum Chemical Corporation
99 Park Avenue
New York, NY 10016
(212) 551–0438

Description: Support to colleges, universities and private secondary and elementary schools, mainly through matching gift programs; funding focused generally near headquarters and operating locations
$ Given: $850,000 corporate giving total; amount to education not specified
Contact: Arden Melick, Director, Corporate Communications

Republic New York Corporation
452 5th Avenue
New York, NY 10018
(212) 525–6597

Description: Funding for private pre–college education, principally in the New York City metropolitan area
$ Given: $1,000,000 corporate giving total; amount to education not specified
Contact: J. Phillips Burgess, Vice President, Director of Corporate Communications

Revlon
Revlon Foundation
767 5th Avenue
New York, NY 10153
(212) 572–5000

Description: Funding provided nationally and in locations where company has operating divisions
$ Given: Of $4,084,447 corporate giving total, 30% designated for education
Contact: Phyllis Orta, Manager, Community Relations

United States Trust Company of New York
United States Trust Company of New York Foundation
114 W. 47th Street
New York, NY 10036
(212) 852–1330

Description: Funding focused primarily in the metropolitan New York City area
$ Given: Of $525,000 corporate giving total, 20–30% designated for education
Contact: Carol Strickland, Vice President & Secretary

NORTH CAROLINA

Burlington Industries, Inc.
Burlington Industries Foundation
3330 W. Friendly Avenue
P.O. Box 21207
Greensboro, NC 27420
(919) 379–2515

Description: Matching grants awarded; funding provided primarily in North and South Carolina, Virginia, and near operating locations
$ Given: Grants range from $1,000 to $10,000; of $1,000,000 corporate giving total, 65% designated for education
Contact: Park R. Davidson, Executive Director; or local plant manager

Burroughs Wellcome Company
Burroughs Wellcome Fund
3030 Cornwallis Road
Research Triangle Park, NC 27709
(919) 248–4177

Description: Focus on encouraging students toward careers in science and medicine; funding provided nationally, with emphasis on North Carolina
$ Given: Of $16,000,000 corporate giving total, 15% designated for education
Contact: Martha G. Peck, Fund Executive Director

Duke Power Company
Duke Power Company Foundation
P.O. Box 33189
Charlotte, NC 28242
(704) 373–3224

Description: Education monies given to private pre-college education; funding focused primarily near headquarters and operating locations
$ Given: Of $5,200,000 corporate giving total, 35–40% designated for education
Contact: Robert Allen, Director, Corporate Contributions

Glaxo, Inc.
Glaxo Foundation
5 Moore Drive
Research Triangle Park, NC 27709
(919) 248–2588

Description: Funding provided principally near headquarters and operating locations
$ Given: $2,325,099 corporate giving total; amount to education not specified

OHIO

American Financial Corporation
American Financial Corporation Foundation
One East Fourth Street
Cincinnati, OH
(513) 579–2400

Description: Emphasis on Cincinnati area
$ Given: Of $2,472,572 corporate giving total, 15% designated for education
Contact: Sandra W. Heimann, Secretary

Borden
Borden Foundation
180 E. Broad Street
Columbus, OH 43215
(614) 225–4340

Description: Preference given to locations where Borden, Inc. maintains facilities
$ Given: Of $3,100,000 corporate giving total, 25–30% designated for education
Contact: Judy Barker, President

BP America, Inc.
200 Public Square, 35–A
Cleveland, OH 44114
(216) 586–8625

Description: Highest priorities are scientific, mathematical and technical education at both collegiate and pre-collegiate levels; funding provided primarily near corporate operating locations and to national organizations
$ Given: Grant awards range from $5,000 to $50,000; of $13,000,000 corporate giving total, 35–40% designated for education
Contact: Lance C. Buhl, Manager, Corporate Contributions

Cleveland Electric Illuminating Company
Centerior Energy Foundation
P.O. Box 5000, Room 631
Cleveland, OH 44101
(216) 622–9800

Description: Grant monies given to education in private high schools; employee matching gifts program; funding provided exclusively in Northeast Ohio
$ Given: Grants range from $1,000—$10,000; of $1,408,735 corporate giving total, 15–20% designated for education

Dana Corporation
Dana Corporation Foundation
P.O. Box 1000
Toledo, OH 43697
(419) 535–4520

Description: Funding for private pre-college education, primarily where Dana Corporation maintains operating facilities; national organizations also funded
$ Given: Of $2,200,000 corporate giving total, 20–25% designated for education
Contact: Robert Cowie, Vice President

Eaton Corporation
Eaton Charitable Fund
Eaton Center
Cleveland, OH 44114
(216) 523–4822

Description: Corporate operating locations receive highest priority; no grants for operating support to educational institutions or to their scholarship or endowment funds
$ Given: Of $4,000,000 corporate giving total, 35–40% designated for education
Contact: Frederick B. Unger, Director, Community Affairs

Federated Department Stores
Robert Campeau Family Foundation (U.S.)
7 West 7th Street
Cincinnati, OH 45202
(513) 579–7166

Description: Support to private schools for children and young adults with learning disabilities; funding provided near headquarters and operating locations only
$ Given: Of $7,000,000 corporate giving total, 20–25% designated for education
Contact: Patricia A. Ikeda, Executive Director

Forrest City Enterprises
Forrest City Enterprises Charitable Foundation
10800 Brookpark Road
Cleveland, OH 44130
(216) 267–1200

Description: Funding to religious and other private education programs; funding focused in company operating locations, primarily in the Cleveland and New York City areas
$ Given: Of $507,632 corporate giving total, 25–30% designated for education
Contact: Nate Shafran, Treasurer

GenCorp
GenCorp Foundation
175 Ghent Road
Fairlawn, OH 44313
(216) 869–4298

Description: Funding provided near corporate operating locations
$ Given: Of $1,000,000 corporate giving total, 25% designated for education
Contact: Karen Imgram, Director of Community Relations

Lubrizol Corporation
Lubrizol Foundation
29425 Chagrin Boulevard
Suite 303
Pepper Lake, OH 44122
(216) 943–4200

Description: Much support awarded through a matching gifts program for higher and secondary education; funding provided near headquarters and operating locations only
$ Given: Of $1,000,000 corporate giving total, 35–40% designated for education
Contact: Douglas W. Richardson, President & Chief Operating Officer

National City Corporation
National City Corporation
Bank Charitable
Contributions Trust
c/o Public Affairs Dept.
National City Bank
P.O. Box 5756
Cleveland, OH 44101
(216) 575–2000

Description: Support for private, pre–college education; program to match employee contributions to education; funding focused mainly in Cleveland, Ohio, in Nebraska and Ohio operating locations, and in parts of Kentucky and Indiana; national organizations considered on an individual basis
$ Given: Of $4,900,000 of corporate giving total, 20–25% designated for education
Contact: Allen C. Waddle, Senior Vice President

Ohio Bell Telephone Company
Ohio Bell Foundation
45 Erieview Plaza
Room 870
Cleveland, OH 44114
(216) 822–2423

Description: Employee matching gifts program; funding provided to Ohio–based organizations
$ Given: Of $2,763,000 corporate giving total, 30% designated for education

Ohio Mattress Company
Wuliger Foundation
130 E. 9th Street
Cleveland, OH 44114
(216) 522–1310

Description: Limited private support; funding focused primarily in Ohio
$ Given: Of $1,500,000 corporate giving total, 35–40% designated for education
Contact: Ernest Wuliger, President

Owens Corning Fiberglas Corporation
Owens Corning Foundation
Fiberglas Tower
Toledo, OH 43659
(419) 248–8315

Description: Funding limited to private pre–college education near headquarters and operating locations only
$ Given: Of $1,155,200 corporate giving total, 35% designated for education
Contact: Emerson J. Ross, Secretary, Corporate Contributions

Parker–Hannifin Corporation
Parker–Hannifin Foundation
17325 Euclid Avenue
Cleveland, OH 44112
(216) 531–3000

Description: National support to student aid
$ Given: Of $1,650,000 corporate giving total, 20% designated for education
Contact: Joseph D. Whiteman

Reliance Electric Company
Reliance Electric Company
Charitable Scientific &
Educational Trust
6065 Parkland Boulevard
Cleveland, OH 44124
(216) 266-1923

Description: Funding provided in operating locations with emphasis on Cleveland, Ohio
$ Given: Of $750,000 corporate giving total, 40–45% designated for education
Contact: William C. Gallagher, Secretary

Star Bank, N.A.
Star Bank, N.A. Cincinnati
Foundation
P.O. Box 1038
Cincinnati, OH 45201
(513) 632-4524

Description: Giving emphasis on Cincinnati and the state of Ohio
$ Given: Of $500,000 corporate giving total, 10–15% designated for education
Contact: David Bowen, Vice President, Public Affairs

TRINOVA Corporation
TRINOVA Foundation
3000 Strayer
P.O. Box 50
Maumee, OH 43537-0050
(419) 867-2294

Description: Funding provided near headquarters and operating locations only
$ Given: $700,000 corporate giving total; amount to education not specified
Contact: Contributions Administrator

OKLAHOMA

Occidental Oil & Gas Corporation
Occidental Oil & Gas
Charitable Foundation
Box 300
Tulsa, OK 74102
(918) 561-2212

Description: Funding provided nationally in locations where Occidental Oil & Gas Corporation has business operations
$ Given: Of $630,000 corporate giving total, 35–40% designated for education
Contact: Ronald G. Peters, Executive Secretary

Williams Companies
Williams Companies
Foundation
P.O. Box 2400
Tulsa, OK 74102
(918) 588-2106

Description: Funding for private education, exclusively in areas near company headquarters and operating locations
$ Given: Of $2,048,945 corporate giving total, 15–20% designated for education
Contact: Hannah Davis Robson, Manager

OREGON

Tektronix
Tektronix Foundation
P.O. Box 500
Beaverton, OR 97077
(503) 627–7085

Description: Funding for private education in Northwest Oregon and Southwest Washington
$ Given: Of $2,000,000 corporate giving total, 65–70% designated for education
Contact: Diana Smiley, Executive Director

PENNSYLVANIA

AMETEK
AMETEK Foundation
Station Square #2
Paoli, PA 19301
(215) 647–2121

Description: Funding to national organizations near plant locations
$ Given: Of $1,200,000 corporate giving total, 30–35% designated for education
Contact: Robert W. Yannarell, Assistant Secretary

AMP
AMP Foundation
P.O. Box 3608
Harrisburg, PA 17105
(717) 780–6708

Description: Grant monies given to private education within a 50–mile radius of Harrisburg, Pennsylvania and operating locations
$ Given: Of $775,000 corporate giving total, 45–50% designated for education
Contact: Merrill A. Yohe, Chair, Contributions Committee

Consolidated Natural Gas Company
Consolidated Natural Gas Foundation
CNG Tower
Pittsburgh, PA 15222–3199
(412) 227–1185

Description: Funding provided principally in company's service area of Western Pennsylvania, Ohio, Virginia and West Virginia; to a lesser extent in Louisiana, Oklahoma and Washington, D.C.
$ Given: Of $3,300,000 corporate giving total, 30% designated for education
Contact: Ray N. Ivey

Harsco Corporation
Harsco Corporation Fund
P.O. Box 8888
Camp Hill, PA 17011
(717) 763–7064

Description: Two–fifths of education monies awarded in a single grant to the National Merit Scholarship Corporation for scholarships to children of employees; funding provided near headquarters and operating locations only
$ Given: Of $550,000 corporate giving total, 35–40% designated for education
Contact: Robert Yokum, Secretary

H.J. Heinz Company
H.J. Heinz Company Foundation
P.O. Box 57
Pittsburgh, PA 15230
(412) 456–5772

Description: Support for minority and private college and pre–college education; funding focused in areas where H.J. Heinz Company maintains facilities
$ Given: Of $5,000,000 corporate giving total, 35–40% designated for education
Contact: Loretta M. Oken, Administrator

Hunt Manufacturing Company
Hunt Manufacturing Company Foundation
230 S. Broad Street
Philadelphia, PA 19102
(215) 732–7700

Description: Funding for a limited number of elementary and secondary level projects involving curriculum development, specific skills training, or education innovation; funding provided to organizations in the following communities: Greater Philadelphia region; Iredell County, North Carolina; Florence, Alabama; Fresno, California; and Florence, Kentucky
$ Given: Of $635,000 corporate giving total, 15% designated for education
Contact: William E. Parshall, Secretary

Pennwalt Corporation
Atochen North American Foundation
Three Parkway
Philadelphia, PA 19102
(215) 587–7653

Description: Scholarships to children of employees; funding provided nationally with emphasis on areas where Pennwalt has operations
$ Given: Grants range from $1,000 to $5,000; of $1,000,000 corporate giving total, 30–35% designated for education
Contact: George L. Nagar

Pittsburgh National Bank
Pittsburgh National Bank Foundation
5th Avenue & Wood Street
Pittsburgh, PA 15222
(412) 762–4222

Description: Support for public and private college and pre–college education; funding provided in metropolitan Pittsburgh and surrounding communities of Allegheny County
$ Given: Of $1,700,000 corporate giving total, 15–20% designated for education
Contact: D. Paul Beard, Secretary, Distribution Committee

PPG Industries
PPG Industries Foundation
One PPG Place
Pittsburgh, PA 15272
(412) 434–2962

Description: National support for private secondary education with emphasis on corporate operating locations; special interest in Pittsburgh, Pennsylvania area
$ Given: Of $5,000,000 corporate giving total, 25–30% designated for education
Contact: Roslyn Rosenblatt, Executive Director

Rohm & Hass Company
Independence Mall West
Philadelphia, PA 19105
(215) 592–2863

Description: Matching gifts for pre–college education; funding focused primarily in communities where employees live and company has facilities
$ Given: Of $4,800,000 corporate giving total, 45–50% designated for education
Contact: Delbert S. Payne, Manager, Corporate Social Investment Program

RHODE ISLAND

Fleet National Bank
Fleet Charitable Trust
111 Westminister Street
Providence, RI 02903
(401) 278–6242

Description: Interests include public and private secondary education and scholarships; funding limited almost exclusively to the State of Rhode Island
$ Given: Of $1,200,000 corporate giving total, 50% designated for education
Contact: Sheila McDonald, Secretary

Textron
Textron Charitable Trust
P.O. Box 878
Providence, RI 02901
(401) 457–2430

Description: One–half of education monies given in matching grants; funding focused primarily in areas where company operates
$ Given: Of $3,000,000 corporate giving total, 30–35% designated for education
Contact: Elizabeth W. Monahan

SOUTH CAROLINA

Citizens & Southern National Bank of South Carolina
Citizens & Southern
National Bank of South
Carolina Foundation
P.O. Box 727
Columbia, SC 29222
(803) 765–8011

Description: Majority goes to South Carolina Foundation of Independent Colleges; scholarships awarded to children of employees and to private pre–college education; given in South Carolina, particularly in areas served by the corporation
$ Given: Of $1,300,000 corporate giving total, 30–35% designated for education
Contact: Robert V. Royall, Jr., Chair

Springs Industries
P.O. Box 70
Fort Mill, SC 29715
(803) 547–3650

Description: Support for private pre–college education; funding provided principally near operating locations, and to national organizations
$ Given: Of $900,000 corporate giving total, 60% designated for education
Contact: Robert L. Thompson, Jr., Vice President, Public Affairs

TEXAS

ENRON Corporation
ENRON Foundation
P.O. Box 1188
Houston, TX 77251–1188
(713) 853–5400

Description: Support for private secondary education; funding provided near headquarters and operating locations only
$ Given: Of $4,000,000 corporate giving total, 25–30% designated for education
Contact: Deborah Christie

First City Bank Corporation of Texas
P.O. Box 2557
Houston, TX 77252
(713) 658–6109

Description: Support to Texas-based organizations and programs serving bank communities
$ Given: Of $1,200,000 corporate giving total, 10–15% designated for education
Contact: Jim Day, Senior Vice President, Public Relations

LTV Corporation
LTV Foundation
P.O. Box 655003
Dallas, TX 75265–5003
(214) 979–7726

Description: Funding provided principally near operating locations and to national organizations
$ Given: Of $1,100,000 corporate giving total, 15% designated for education
Contact: Brent Berryman, Executive Director

Panhandle Eastern Corporation
P.O. Box 2521
Houston, TX 77252
(713) 759–3580

Description: Education second priority; matching gifts program to private secondary schools; funding focused primarily in Houston metropolitan area
$ Given: $2,500,000 corporate giving total; amount to education not specified
Contact: Marla Bernard, Manager, Community Relations

Shell Oil Company
Shell Oil Company Foundation
Two Shell Plaza, Box 2099
Houston, TX 77252
(713) 241–3617

Description: Matching gifts program and scholarships for children of employees; funding provided nationally with emphasis on communities where Shell employees are located
$ Given: Of $20,000,000 corporate giving total, 60% designated for education
Contact: Doris J. O'Connor, Senior Vice President

Texas Instruments
Texas Instruments Foundation
P.O. Box 655474, M/S 271
Dallas, TX 75265
(214) 995–3172

Description: Support for private education nationally, with emphasis on Texas-based groups
$ Given: $10,400,000 corporate giving total; amount to education not specified
Contact: Linda Coumelis, Manager, Corporate Community Relations

VIRGINIA

Dominion Bankshares Corporation
Dominion Bankshares Corporation Charitable Trust
P.O. Box 13327
Roanoke, VA 24040
(703) 563–7595

$ Given: $1,400,000 corporate giving total
Contact: Edward M. Newman, Vice President & Adminstrator

Ethyl Corporation
330 S. Fourth Street
P.O. Box 2189
Richmond, VA 23217
(804) 788–5413

Description: Support for public and private institutions, with emphasis on those which serve as potential sources of employees or are of significance to employee family members; support for secondary level study; funding provided near headquarters and operating locations only
$ Given: Of $3,200,000 corporate giving total, 40–45% designated for education
Contact: A. Prescott Rowe, Vice President, Corporate Communications

Sovran Bank, N.A.
Sovran Foundation
Trust Department
P.O. Box 26903
Richmond, VA 23261
(804) 788–2963

Description: Funding provided in communities serviced by bank
$ Given: Of $2,000,000 corporate giving total, 15–20% designated for education
Contact: Elizabeth D. Seaman, Secretary & Treasurer

CORPORATE/EMPLOYEE PROGRAMS

• • • • • • • • • • • • • • • • • • • •

WASHINGTON

The Boeing Company
Boeing Company
Charitable Trust
7755 East Marginal Way So.
Seattle, WA 98108
(206) 655–6679

Description: Education gifts highest priority; given near corporate operating locations, primarily in Philadelphia, Pennsylvania; Wichita, Kansas; and Seattle, Washington
$ Given: $23,000,000 corporate giving total; amount to education not specified
Contact: Joe A. Taller, Director, Public and Community Affairs

PACCAR
PACCAR Foundation
P.O. Box 1518
Bellevue, WA 98009
(206) 455–7400

Description: Funding for private education near headquarters and operating locations only
$ Given: Of $1,603,151 corporate giving total, 30–35% designated for education
Contact: Edgar A. Carpenter, Vice President & Treasurer

Simpson Investment Company
Matlock Foundation
1201 Third Avenue
Suite 4900
Seattle, WA 98101–3009
(206) 224–5196

Description: Substantial support to secondary schools, especially private schools; funding provided in Washington, Oregon, California, Michigan, Ohio, Pennsylvania, Texas and Vermont
$ Given: Of $2,000,000 corporate giving total, 15–20% designated for education
Contact: Lin Smith

Skinner Corporation
Skinner Foundation
1326 5th Avenue, No. 711
Seattle, WA 98101
(206) 623–6480

Description: Support provided in Washington, Oregon, Idaho, Alaska and Hawaii
$ Given: Of $603,038 corporate giving total, 15–20% designated for education
Contact: Sandra Fry, Administrator

Weyerhaeuser Company
Weyerhaeuser Company Foundation
CHIF31
Tacoma, WA 98477
(206) 924–3159

Description: Funding provided nationally and internationally to private pre-college schools; emphasis on communities, particularly remote communities, in which company has a significant number of employees
$ Given: Of $6,255,310 corporate giving total, 41% designated for education
Contact: Mary S. Hall, President

WISCONSIN

Bucyrus–Erie
Bucyrus–Erie Foundation
P.O. Box 500
South Milwaukee, WI
53172–0500
(414) 768–5005

Description: Funding focused primarily in Milwaukee, Wisconsin, and communities where company has business operations or subsidiaries
$ Given: Of $900,000 corporate giving total, 30–35% designated for education
Contact: Dennis L. Strawderman, Manager & Secretary

Consolidated Papers
Consolidated Papers Foundation
Box 8050
Wisconsin Rapids, WI 54495
(715) 422–3368

Description: Support mostly to universities; merit scholarship programs; funding focused near headquarters and operating locations
$ Given: Of $877,000 corporate giving total, 65–70% designated for education
Contact: Daniel P. Meyer, President

S.C. Johnson & Son
Johnson's Wax Fund
1525 Howe Street
Racine, WI 53403
(414) 631–2267

Description: Scholarships for children of employees; support for high school funding; some gifts given nationally, but primarily in Wisconsin and the Midwest
$ Given: Of $2,156,653 corporate giving total, 50–55% designated for education
Contact: Reva Holmes, Vice President & Secretary

Marshall & Ilsley Bank
Marshall & Ilsley Bank Foundation
770 N. Water Street
Milwaukee, WI 53201
(414) 765–7835

Description: Scholarships and scholarship funds; giving focused primarily in Wisconsin, with emphasis on Milwaukee
$ Given: Of $917,225 corporate giving total, 25–30% designated for education
Contact: Diana L. Sebion, Secretary

National Presto Industries
Presto Foundation
3925 N. Hastings Way
Eau Claire, WI 54703
(715) 839–2121

Description: Scholarships to children of employees; funding provided in Northwest Wisconsin, especially in Eau Claire and Chippewa County, and in operating locations
$ Given: Grants range from $100 to $5,000; of $553,530 corporate giving total, 15–20% designated for education
Contact: Norma Jaenke, Executive Director

Wisconsin Energy Corporation
Wisconsin Energy Corporation Foundation
231 W. Michigan Street
P.O. Box 2046
Milwaukee, WI 53201
(414) 221–2105

Description: Support for private education, almost exclusively in company's service area; grants may be made in other states
$ Given: Of $2,700,000 corporate giving total, 20–25% designated for education

Special Population Funding

The following chapter on "Special Population Funding" covers private school funding assistance available to children and families in special categories. These categories include: American Indians, developmentally disabled children, children of migratory workers, and other populations, such as gifted, minority, and disadvantaged students.

American Indian parents and children should be aware that education grants are generally made to communities and schools, not directly to individual students. Award figures cited in this section reflect this fact. For national information about any of the education funding programs for American Indians, you may contact Aaron Neal Shedd in Washington, D.C. at (202) 732-1887.

Parents of developmentally disabled children may be interested to know that a range of $450,000 to $5million is available nationwide for elementary and secondary schooling. Applications for funding must be made through state agencies. Readers should be aware that, on a national level, approximately $285million are available to address the needs of children of migratory workers. The six miscellaneous entries are listed in alphabetical order, as they may be applicable to students nationwide.

SPECIAL POPULATION FUNDING

• • • • • • • • • • • • • • • • • • • •

FUNDING FOR AMERICAN INDIANS

(Only parents of qualified children may apply)

ALASKA

Alaska Indian Education - Special Projects
Anchorage Agency
P.O. Box 100120
Anchorage, AK 99510
(907) 271-4088

Description: Funding to provide better educational services to American Indian children and to reduce the dropout rate
$ Given: $143,000 per community, with a range of $50,000 to $350,000 per award
Who May Apply: Individuals, including parents

Education Grants to Indian-Controlled Schools in Alaska
Anchorage Agency
P.O. Box 100120
Anchorage, AK 99510
(907) 271-4088

Description: Financial assistance to Indian-controlled schools to meet the needs of American Indian children
$ Given: $175,000 per school, with a range of $82,000 to $366,000 per award
Who May Apply: Parents, tribal groups and other interested and qualified parties

ARIZONA

Arizona Indian Education - Special Projects
Colorado River Agency
Route 1, Box C
Parker, AZ
(602) 669-2134

Description: Funding to provide better educational services to American Indian children and to reduce the dropout rate
$ Given: $143,000 per community, with a range of $50,000 to $350,000 per award
Who May Apply: Individuals, including parents

Education Grants to Indian-Controlled Schools in Arizona
Colorado River Agency
Route 1, Box C
Parker, AZ
(602) 669-2134

Description: Financial assistance to Indian-controlled schools to meet the needs of American Indian children
$ Given: $175,000 per school, with a range of $82,000 to $366,000 per award
Who May Apply: Parents, tribal groups and other interested and qualified parties

CALIFORNIA

California Indian Education - Special Projects
Central California Agency
1800 Tribute Road
P.O. Box 15740
Sacramento, CA 95813
(916) 484-4357

Description: Funding to provide better educational services to American Indian children and to reduce the dropout rate
$ Given: $143,000 per community, with a range of $50,000 to $350,000 per award
Who May Apply: Individuals, including parents

Education Grants to Indian-Controlled Schools in California
Central California Agency
1800 Tribute Road
P.O. Box 15740
Sacramento, CA 95813
(916) 484-4357

Description: Financial assistance to Indian-controlled schools to meet the needs of American Indian children
$ Given: $175,000 per school, with a range of $82,000 to $366,000 per award
Who May Apply: Parents, tribal groups and other interested and qualified parties

COLORADO

Colorado Indian Education - Special Projects
Ute Agency
Towaoc, CO 81334
(303) 565-8471

Description: Funding to provide better educational services to American Indian children and to reduce the dropout rate
$ Given: $143,000 per community, with a range of $50,000 to $350,000 per award
Who May Apply: Individuals, including parents

Education Grants to Indian-Controlled Schools in Colorado
Ute Agency
Towaoc, CO 81334
(303) 565-8471

Description: Financial assistance to Indian-controlled schools to meet the needs of American Indian children
$ Given: $175,000 per school, with a range of $82,000 to $366,000 per award
Who May Apply: Parents, tribal groups and other interested and qualified parties

FLORIDA

Florida Indian Education - Special Projects
Seminole Agency
6075 Stirling Road
Hollywood, FL 33024
(305) 581-7050

Description: Funding to provide better educational services to American Indian children and to reduce the dropout rate
$ Given: $143,000 per community, with a range of $50,000 to $350,000 per award
Who May Apply: Individuals, including parents

Education Grants to Indian-Controlled Schools in Florida
Seminole Agency
6075 Stirling Road
Hollywood, FL 33024
(305) 581-7050

Description: Financial assistance to Indian-controlled schools to meet the needs of American Indian children
$ Given: $175,000 per school, with a range of $82,000 to $366,000 per award
Who May Apply: Parents, tribal groups and other interested and qualified parties

IDAHO

Idaho Indian Education - Special Projects
Fort Hall Agency
Fort hall, ID 83203
(208) 237-0600

Description: Funding to provide better educational services to American Indian children and to reduce the dropout rate
$ Given: $143,000 per community, with a range of $50,000 to $350,000 per award
Who May Apply: Individuals, including parents

Education Grants to Indian-Controlled Schools in Idaho
Fort Hall Agency
Fort hall, ID 83203
(208) 237-0600

Description: Financial assistance to Indian-controlled schools to meet the needs of American Indian children
$ Given: $175,000 per school, with a range of $82,000 to $366,000 per award
Who May Apply: Parents, tribal groups and other interested and qualified parties

IOWA

Iowa Indian Education - Special Projects
Sac & Fox Area Field Office
Tama, IA 52339
(515) 484-4041

Description: Funding to provide better educational services to American Indian children and to reduce the dropout rate
$ Given: $143,000 per community, with a range of $50,000 to $350,000 per award
Who May Apply: Individuals, including parents

Education Grants to Indian-Controlled Schools in Iowa
Sac & Fox Area Field Office
Tama, IA 52339
(515) 484-4041

Description: Financial assistance to Indian-controlled schools to meet the needs of American Indian children
$ Given: $175,000 per school, with a range of $82,000 to $366,000 per award
Who May Apply: Parents, tribal groups and other interested and qualified parties

KANSAS

Kansas Indian Education - Special Projects
Horton Agency
Horton, KS 66439
(913) 486-2161

Description: Funding to provide better educational services to American Indian children and to reduce the dropout rate
$ Given: $143,000 per community, with a range of $50,000 to $350,000 per award
Who May Apply: Individuals, including parents

Education Grants to Indian-Controlled Schools in Kansas
Horton Agency
Horton, KS 66439
(913) 486-2161

Description: Financial assistance to Indian-controlled schools to meet the needs of American Indian children
$ Given: $175,000 per school, with a range of $82,000 to $366,000 per award
Who May Apply: Parents, tribal groups and other interested and qualified parties

MINNESOTA

Minnesota Indian Education - Special Projects
Minnesota Agency
P.O. Box 97
Cass Lake, MN 56633
(218) 335-6913

Description: Funding to provide better educational services to American Indian children and to reduce the dropout rate
$ Given: $143,000 per community, with a range of $50,000 to $350,000 per award
Who May Apply: Individuals, including parents

Education Grants to Indian-Controlled Schools in Minnesota
Minnesota Agency
P.O. Box 97
Cass Lake, MN 56633
(218) 335-6913

Description: Financial assistance to Indian-controlled schools to meet the needs of American Indian children
$ Given: $175,000 per school, with a range of $82,000 to $366,000 per award
Who May Apply: Parents, tribal groups and other interested and qualified parties

MISSISSIPPI

Mississippi Indian Education - Special Projects
Choctaw Agency
421 Powell
Philadelphia, MS 39350
(601) 656-1521

Description: Funding to provide better educational services to American Indian children and to reduce the dropout rate
$ Given: $143,000 per community, with a range of $50,000 to $350,000 per award
Who May Apply: Individuals, including parents

Education Grants to Indian-Controlled Schools in Mississippi
Choctaw Agency
421 Powell
Philadelphia, MS 39350
(601) 656-1521

Description: Financial assistance to Indian-controlled schools to meet the needs of American Indian children
$ Given: $175,000 per school, with a range of $82,000 to $366,000 per award
Who May Apply: Parents, tribal groups and other interested and qualified parties

MONTANA

Montana Indian Education - Special Projects
Fort Peck Agency
P.O. Box 637
Poplar, MT 59255
(406) 768-5311

Description: Funding to provide better educational services to American Indian children and to reduce the dropout rate
$ Given: $143,000 per community, with a range of $50,000 to $350,000 per award
Who May Apply: Individuals, including parents

Education Grants to Indian-Controlled Schools in Montana
Fort Peck Agency
P.O. Box 637
Poplar, MT 59255
(406) 768-5311

Description: Financial assistance to Indian-controlled schools to meet the needs of American Indian children
$ Given: $175,000 per school, with a range of $82,000 to $366,000 per award
Who May Apply: Parents, tribal groups and other interested and qualified parties

NEBRASKA

Nebraska Indian Education - Special Projects
Winnebago Agency
Winnebago, NE 68071

Description: Funding to provide better educational services to American Indian children and to reduce the dropout rate
$ Given: $143,000 per community, with a range of $50,000 to $350,000 per award
Who May Apply: Individuals, including parents

Education Grants to Indian-Controlled Schools in Nebraska
Winnebago Agency
Winnebago, NE 68071

Description: Financial assistance to Indian-controlled schools to meet the needs of American Indian children
$ Given: $175,000 per school, with a range of $82,000 to $366,000 per award
Who May Apply: Parents, tribal groups and other interested and qualified parties

NEVADA

Nevada Indian Education - Special Projects
Western Nevada Agency
Stewart, NV 89437
(702) 887-3500

Description: Funding to provide better educational services to American Indian children and to reduce the dropout rate
$ Given: $143,000 per community, with a range of $50,000 to $350,000 per award
Who May Apply: Individuals, including parents

Education Grants to Indian-Controlled Schools in Nevada
Western Nevada Agency
Stewart, NV 89437
(702) 887-3500

Description: Financial assistance to Indian-controlled schools to meet the needs of American Indian children
$ Given: $175,000 per school, with a range of $82,000 to $366,000 per award
Who May Apply: Parents, tribal groups and other interested and qualified parties

NEW MEXICO

New Mexico Indian Education - Special Projects
Pueblos Agency
Federal Building
P.O. Box 849
Santa Fe, NM 87501
(505) 988-6431

Description: Funding to provide better educational services to American Indian children and to reduce the dropout rate
$ Given: $143,000 per community, with a range of $50,000 to $350,000 per award
Who May Apply: Individuals, including parents

Education Grants to Indian-Controlled Schools in New Mexico
Pueblos Agency
Federal Building
P.O. Box 849
Santa Fe, NM 87501
(505) 988-6431

Description: Financial assistance to Indian-controlled schools to meet the needs of American Indian children
$ Given: $175,000 per school, with a range of $82,000 to $366,000 per award
Who May Apply: Parents, tribal groups and other interested and qualified parties

NEW YORK

New York Indian Education - Special Projects
New York Field Office
Federal Building, No 523
100 South Clinton Street
Syracuse, NY 13202
(315) 423-5476

Description: Funding to provide better educational services to American Indian children and to reduce the dropout rate
$ Given: $143,000 per community, with a range of $50,000 to $350,000 per award
Who May Apply: Individuals, including parents

Education Grants to Indian-Controlled Schools in New York
New York Field Office
Federal Building, No 523
100 South Clinton Street
Syracuse, NY 13202
(315) 423-5476

Description: Financial assistance to Indian-controlled schools to meet the needs of American Indian children
$ Given: $175,000 per school, with a range of $82,000 to $366,000 per award
Who May Apply: Parents, tribal groups and other interested and qualified parties

NORTH CAROLINA

North Carolina Indian Education - Special Projects
Cherokee Agency
Cherokee, NC 28719
(704) 497-9131

Description: Funding to provide better educational services to American Indian children and to reduce the dropout rate
$ Given: $143,000 per community, with a range of $50,000 to $350,000 per award
Who May Apply: Individuals, including parents

Education Grants to Indian-Controlled Schools in North Carolina
Cherokee Agency
Cherokee, NC 28719
(704) 497-9131

Description: Financial assistance to Indian-controlled schools to meet the needs of American Indian children
$ Given: $175,000 per school, with a range of $82,000 to $366,000 per award
Who May Apply: Parents, tribal groups and other interested and qualified parties

NORTH DAKOTA

North Dakota Indian Education - Special Projects
Turtle Mountain Agency
Belcourt, ND 58316
(701) 477-3191

Description: Funding to provide better educational services to American Indian children and to reduce the dropout rate
$ Given: $143,000 per community, with a range of $50,000 to $350,000 per award
Who May Apply: Individuals, including parents

Education Grants to Indian-Controlled Schools in North Dakota
Turtle Mountain Agency
Belcourt, ND 58316
(701) 477-3191

Description: Financial assistance to Indian-controlled schools to meet the needs of American Indian children
$ Given: $175,000 per school, with a range of $82,000 to $366,000 per award
Who May Apply: Parents, tribal groups and other interested and qualified parties

OKLAHOMA

Oklahoma Indian Education - Special Projects
Pawnee Agency
P.O. Box 440
Pawnee, OK 74058
(918) 762-2585

Description: Funding to provide better educational services to American Indian children and to reduce the dropout rate
$ Given: $143,000 per community, with a range of $50,000 to $350,000 per award
Who May Apply: Individuals, including parents

Education Grants to Indian-Controlled Schools in Oklahoma
Pawnee Agency
P.O. Box 440
Pawnee, OK 74058
(918) 762-2585

Description: Financial assistance to Indian-controlled schools to meet the needs of American Indian children
$ Given: $175,000 per school, with a range of $82,000 to $366,000 per award
Who May Apply: Parents, tribal groups and other interested and qualified parties

OREGON

Oregon Indian Education - Special Projects
Warm Springs Agency
Warm Springs, OR 97761
(503) 553-1121

Description: Funding to provide better educational services to American Indian children and to reduce the dropout rate
$ Given: $143,000 per community, with a range of $50,000 to $350,000 per award
Who May Apply: Individuals, including parents

Education Grants to Indian-Controlled Schools in Oregon
Warm Springs Agency
Warm Springs, OR 97761
(503) 553-1121

Description: Financial assistance to Indian-controlled schools to meet the needs of American Indian children
$ Given: $175,000 per school, with a range of $82,000 to $366,000 per award
Who May Apply: Parents, tribal groups and other interested and qualified parties

SOUTH DAKOTA

South Dakota Indian Education - Special Projects
Cheyenne River Agency
P.O. Box 325
Eagle Butte, SD 57625
(605) 964-6611

Description: Funding to provide better educational services to American Indian children and to reduce the dropout rate
$ Given: $143,000 per community, with a range of $50,000 to $350,000 per award
Who May Apply: Individuals, including parents

Education Grants to Indian-Controlled Schools in South Dakota
Cheyenne River Agency
P.O. Box 325
Eagle Butte, SD 57625
(605) 964-6611

Description: Financial assistance to Indian-controlled schools to meet the needs of American Indian children
$ Given: $175,000 per school, with a range of $82,000 to $366,000 per award
Who May Apply: Parents, tribal groups and other interested and qualified parties

UTAH

Utah Indian Education - Special Projects
Uintah and Ouray Agency
Fort Duchense, UT 84026
(801) 722-2406

Description: Funding to provide better educational services to American Indian children and to reduce the dropout rate
$ Given: $143,000 per community, with a range of $50,000 to $350,000 per award
Who May Apply: Individuals, including parents

Education Grants to Indian-Controlled Schools in Utah
Uintah and Ouray Agency
Fort Duchense, UT 84026
(801) 722-2406

Description: Financial assistance to Indian-controlled schools to meet the needs of American Indian children
$ Given: $175,000 per school, with a range of $82,000 to $366,000 per award
Who May Apply: Parents, tribal groups and other interested and qualified parties

WASHINGTON

Washington Indian Education - Special Projects
Puget Sound Agency
3006 Colby Avenue
Federal Building
Everett, WA 98201
(206) 258-2651

Description: Funding to provide better educational services to American Indian children and to reduce the dropout rate
$ Given: $143,000 per community, with a range of $50,000 to $350,000 per award
Who May Apply: Individuals, including parents

Education Grants to Indian-Controlled Schools in Washington
Puget Sound Agency
3006 Colby Avenue
Federal Building
Everett, WA 98201
(206) 258-2651

Description: Financial assistance to Indian-controlled schools to meet the needs of American Indian children
$ Given: $175,000 per school, with a range of $82,000 to $366,000 per award
Who May Apply: Parents, tribal groups and other interested and qualified parties

WISCONSIN

Wisconsin Indian Education - Special Projects
Great Lakes Agency
Ashland, Wi 54805
(715) 682-4527

Description: Funding to provide better educational services to American Indian children and to reduce the dropout rate
$ Given: $143,000 per community, with a range of $50,000 to $350,000 per award
Who May Apply: Individuals, including parents

Education Grants to Indian-Controlled Schools in Wisconsin
Great Lakes Agency
Ashland, Wi 54805
(715) 682-4527

Description: Financial assistance to Indian-controlled schools to meet the needs of American Indian children
$ Given: $175,000 per school, with a range of $82,000 to $366,000 per award
Who May Apply: Parents, tribal groups and other interested and qualified parties

WYOMING

Wyoming Indian Education - Special Projects
Wind River Agency
Fort Washakie, WY 82514
(307) 225-8301

Description: Funding to provide better educational services to American Indian children and to reduce the dropout rate
$ Given: $143,000 per community, with a range of $50,000 to $350,000 per award
Who May Apply: Individuals, including parents

Education Grants to Indian-Controlled Schools in Wyoming
Wind River Agency
Fort Washakie, WY 82514
(307) 225-8301

Description: Financial assistance to Indian-controlled schools to meet the needs of American Indian children
$ Given: $175,000 per school, with a range of $82,000 to $366,000 per award
Who May Apply: Parents, tribal groups and other interested and qualified parties

GRANTS FOR THE DEVELOPMENTALLY DISABLED

(Individuals may apply through state agencies)

ALABAMA

Alabama Advocacy Grants for the Developmentally Disabled
Office of Elementary and Secondary Education
State Office Bldg., Rm. 483
501 Dexter Avenue
Montgomery, AL 36130
(205) 261-5156

Description: Grants to support developmentally disabled children and young people in achieving their maximum potential
$ Given: $1,050 to over $10,000 per grant
Contact: Wayne Teague

ALASKA

Alaska Advocacy Grants for the Developmentally Disabled
Office of Elementary and Secondary Education
801 West 10th Street,
P.O. Box F
Juneau, AK 99822
(907) 465-2800

Description: Grants to support developmentally disabled children and young people in achieving their maximum potential
$ Given: $1,000 to $9,500 per grant
Contact: William Demmert

ARIZONA

Arizona Advocacy Grants for the Developmentally Disabled
Office of Elementary and Secondary Education
1535 West Jefferson Street
Phoenix, AZ 85007
(602) 542-4361

Description: Grants to support developmentally disabled children and young people in achieving their maximum potential
$ Given: $2,100 to over $10,000 per grant
Contact: Diane Bishop

ARKANSAS

Arkansas Advocacy Grants for the Developmentally Disabled
Office of Elementary and Secondary Education
4 Capitol Mall, Rm. 304-A
Little Rock, AR 72201
(501) 682-4204

Description: Grants to support developmentally disabled children and young people in achieving their maximum potential
$ Given: $1,200 to $9,200 per grant
Contact: Ruth S Steele

CALIFORNIA

California Advocacy Grants for the Developmentally Disabled
Office of Elementary and Secondary Education
721 Capitol Mall, Rm. 524
P.O. Box 944272
Sacramento, CA 94244
(916) 324-6874

Description: Grants to support developmentally disabled children and young people in achieving their maximum potential
$ Given: $1,050 to $9,700 per grant
Contact: William D Dawson

COLORADO

Colorado Advocacy Grants for the Developmentally Disabled
Office of Elementary and Secondary Education
201 East Colfax
Denver, CO 80203
(303) 866-6806

Description: Grants to support developmentally disabled children and young people in achieving their maximum potential
$ Given: $1,300 to $7,60C per grant
Contact: Ray Kilmer

CONNECTICUT

Connecticut Advocacy Grants for the Developmentally Disabled
Office of Elementary and Secondary Education
165 Capitol Avenue
P.O. Box 2219
Hartford, CT 06145
(203) 566-5061

Description: Grants to support developmentally disabled children and young people in achieving their maximum potential
$ Given: $1,450 to over $8,000 per grant
Contact: Frank Altieri

DELAWARE

Delaware Advocacy Grants for the Developmentally Disabled
Office of Elementary and Secondary Education
P.O. Box 1402
Dover, DE 19903
(302) 736-4601

Description: Grants to support developmentally disabled children and young people in achieving their maximum potential
$ Given: $1,300 to $5,400 per grant
Contact: John J Ryan

FLORIDA

Florida Advocacy Grants for the Developmentally Disabled
Office of Elementary and Secondary Education
The Capitol, Plaza Level 08
Tallahassee, FL 32399
(904) 448-0816

Description: Grants to support developmentally disabled children and young people in achieving their maximum potential
$ Given: $1,250 to $10,300 per grant
Contact: Laurey T Stryker

GEORGIA

Georgia Advocacy Grants for the Developmentally Disabled
Office of Elementary and Secondary Education
205 Butler Street, SE
Atlanta, GA 30334
(404) 656-2800

Description: Grants to support developmentally disabled children and young people in achieving their maximum potential
$ Given: $970 to $6,000 per grant
Contact: Werner Rogers

HAWAII

Hawaii Advocacy Grants for the Developmentally Disabled
Office of Elementary and Secondary Education
1390 Miller Street,
P.O. Box 2360
Honolulu, HI 96804
(808) 548-5972

Description: Grants to support developmentally disabled children and young people in achieving their maximum potential
$ Given: $1,060 to $8,900 per grant
Contact: Kengo Takata

IDAHO

Idaho Advocacy Grants for the Developmentally Disabled
Office of Elementary and Secondary Education
650 West State Street, Room 200
Boise, ID 83720
(208) 334-3301

Description: Grants to support developmentally disabled children and young people in achieving their maximum potential
$ Given: $1,500 to $9,300 per grant
Contact: August Hein

ILLINOIS

Illinois Advocacy Grants for the Developmentally Disabled
Office of Elementary and Secondary Education
100 North First Street
Springfield, IL 62777
(217) 782-3371

Description: Grants to support developmentally disabled children and young people in achieving their maximum potential
$ Given: $1,400 to $9,700 per grant
Contact: Dorothy Maggett

INDIANA

Indiana Advocacy Grants for the Developmentally Disabled
Office of Elementary and Secondary Education
State House, Room 229
Indianapolis, IN 46204
(317) 269-9406

Description: Grants to support developmentally disabled children and young people in achieving their maximum potential
$ Given: $1,250 to $6,700 per grant
Contact: Robert Dalton

IOWA

Iowa Advocacy Grants for the Developmentally Disabled
Office of Elementary and Secondary Education
Grimes State Office Bldg.
Des Moines, IA 50319
(515) 281-6731

Description: Grants to support developmentally disabled children and young people in achieving their maximum potential
$ Given: $1,000 to $8,200 per grant
Contact: Sue Donielson

KANSAS

Kansas Advocacy Grants for the Developmentally Disabled
Office of Elementary and Secondary Education
120 East 10th Street
Topeka, KS 66612
(913) 296-2303

Description: Grants to support developmentally disabled children and young people in achieving their maximum potential
$ Given: $1,600 to $10,500 per grant
Contact: Sharon Freden

KENTUCKY

Kentucky Advocacy Grants for the Developmentally Disabled
Office of Elementary and Secondary Education
Capitol Tower Plaza, 1st Fl.
Frankfort, KY 40601
(502) 564-4770

Description: Grants to support developmentally disabled children and young people in achieving their maximum potential
$ Given: $980 to $8,200 per grant
Contact: Daniel Branham

LOUISIANA

Louisiana Advocacy Grants for the Developmentally Disabled
Office of Elementary and Secondary Education
P.O. Box 94064
Baton Rouge, LA 70804
(504) 342-3602

Description: Grants to support developmentally disabled children and young people in achieving their maximum potential
$ Given: $1,000 to $9,700 per grant
Contact: Wilmer Cody

MAINE

Maine Advocacy Grants for the Developmentally Disabled
Office of Elementary and Secondary Education
State House, Station 23
Augusta, ME 04333
(207) 289-5800

Description: Grants to support developmentally disabled children and young people in achieving their maximum potential
$ Given: $1,400 to $9,300 per grant
Contact: Richard Card

MARYLAND

Maryland Advocacy Grants for the Developmentally Disabled
Office of Elementary and Secondary Education
200 West Baltimore Street
Baltimore, MD 21201
(301) 333-2100

Description: Grants to support developmentally disabled children and young people in achieving their maximum potential
$ Given: $1,250 to $8,900 per grant
Contact: Claud Kitchens

MASSACHUSETTS

Massachusetts Advocacy Grants for the Developmentally Disabled
Office of Elementary and Secondary Education
1385 Hancock Street
Quincy, MA 02169
(617) 770-7200

Description: Grants to support developmentally disabled children and young people in achieving their maximum potential
$ Given: $1,450 to $10,200 per grant
Contact: Fred Williams

MICHIGAN

Michigan Advocacy Grants for the Developmentally Disabled
Office of Elementary and Secondary Education
P.O. Box 30008
Lansing, MI 48909
(517) 335-3537

Description: Grants to support developmentally disabled children and young people in achieving their maximum potential
$ Given: $1,330 to $10,300 per grant
Contact: Douglas Roberts

MINNESOTA

Minnesota Advocacy Grants for the Developmentally Disabled
Office of Elementary and Secondary Education
550 Cedar Street
St Paul, MN 55101
(612) 297-3115

Description: Grants to support developmentally disabled children and young people in achieving their maximum potential
$ Given: $1,400 to $10,550 per grant
Contact: Robert Wedl

MISSISSIPPI

Mississippi Advocacy Grants for the Developmentally Disabled
Office of Elementary and Secondary Education
550 High Street, Room 501
Jackson, MS 39205
(601) 359-3513

Description: Grants to support developmentally disabled children and young people in achieving their maximum potential
$ Given: $950 to $7,000 per grant
Contact: Thomas Saterfiel

MISSOURI

Missouri Advocacy Grants for the Developmentally Disabled
Office of Elementary and Secondary Education
205 Jefferson Street
Jefferson City, MO 65102
(314) 751-4446

Description: Grants to support developmentally disabled children and young people in achieving their maximum potential
$ Given: $1,000 to $10,000 per grant
Contact: Robert Bartman

MONTANA

Montana Advocacy Grants for the Developmentally Disabled
Office of Elementary and Secondary Education
Capitol Building, Room 106
Helena, MT 59620
(406) 444-3654

Description: Grants to support developmentally disabled children and young people in achieving their maximum potential
$ Given: $1,000 to $8,500 per grant
Contact: Jack Copps

NEBRASKA

Nebraska Advocacy Grants for the Developmentally Disabled
Office of Elementary and Secondary Education
301 Centennial Mall, South
Lincoln, NE 68509
(402) 471-2465

Description: Grants to support developmentally disabled children and young people in achieving their maximum potential
$ Given: $1,350 to $9,500 per grant
Contact: Larry Vontz

NEVADA

Nevada Advocacy Grants for the Developmentally Disabled
Office of Elementary and Secondary Education
400 West King Street
Carson City, NV 89710
(702) 885-3104

Description: Grants to support developmentally disabled children and young people in achieving their maximum potential
$ Given: $1,100 to $10,000 per grant
Contact: Marcia Bandera

NEW HAMPSHIRE

New Hampshire Advocacy Grants for the Developmentally Disabled
Office of Elementary and Secondary Education
101 Pleasant Street
Concord, NH 03301
(603) 271-3145

Description: Grants to support developmentally disabled children and young people in achieving their maximum potential
$ Given: $1,300 to $9,700 per grant
Contact: Charles Marston

NEW JERSEY

New Jersey Advocacy Grants for the Developmentally Disabled
Office of Elementary and Secondary Education
225 West State Street
Trenton, NJ 08625
(609) 292-4450

Description: Grants to support developmentally disabled children and young people in achieving their maximum potential
$ Given: $1,500 to $10,400 per grant
Contact: Saul Cooperman

NEW MEXICO

New Mexico Advocacy Grants for the Developmentally Disabled
Office of Elementary and Secondary Education
300 Don Gaspar Avenue
Santa Fe, NM 87501
(505) 827-6635

Description: Grants to support developmentally disabled children and young people in achieving their maximum potential
$ Given: $1,250 to $10,000 per grant
Contact: Alan Morgan

NEW YORK

New York Advocacy Grants for the Developmentally Disabled
Office of Elementary and Secondary Education
Education Building Annex
Albany, NY 12234
(518) 474-4688

Description: Grants to support developmentally disabled children and young people in achieving their maximum potential
$ Given: $1,700 to $10,550 per grant
Contact: Laurence Gloecker

NORTH CAROLINA

North Carolina Advocacy Grants for the Developmentally Disabled
Office of Elementary and Secondary Education
116 West Edenton Street
Raleigh, NC 27603
(919) 733-3813

Description: Grants to support developmentally disabled children and young people in achieving their maximum potential
$ Given: $950 to $8,700 per grant
Contact: William Peek

NORTH DAKOTA

North Dakota Advocacy Grants for the Developmentally Disabled
Office of Elementary and Secondary Education
State Capitol
Bismarck, ND 58505
(701) 224-2260

Description: Grants to support developmentally disabled children and young people in achieving their maximum potential
$ Given: $900 to $9,500 per grant
Contact: Ron Stastney

OHIO

Ohio Advocacy Grants for the Developmentally Disabled
Office of Elementary and Secondary Education
65 South Front Street, Room 808
Columbus, OH 43215
(614) 466-3708

Description: Grants to support developmentally disabled children and young people in achieving their maximum potential
$ Given: $1,350 to $10,400 per grant
Contact: Irene Bandy

OKLAHOMA

Oklahoma Advocacy Grants for the Developmentally Disabled
Office of Elementary and Secondary Education
2500 North Lincoln Boulevard, Room 121
Oklahoma City, OK 73105
(405) 521-3301

Description: Grants to support developmentally disabled children and young people in achieving their maximum potential
$ Given: $1,200 to $8,750 per grant
Contact: Judy Leach

OREGON

Oregon Advocacy Grants for the Developmentally Disabled
Office of Elementary and Secondary Education
700 Pringle Parkway, SE
Salem, OR 97310
(503) 378-8518

Description: Grants to support developmentally disabled children and young people in achieving their maximum potential
$ Given: $1,100 to $10,550 per grant
Contact: Ronald Burge

PENNSYLVANIA

Pennsylvania Advocacy Grants for the Developmentally Disabled
Office of Elementary and Secondary Education
333 Market Street, 10th Fl.
Harrisburg, PA 17126
(717) 787-5820

Description: Grants to support developmentally disabled children and young people in achieving their maximum potential
$ Given: $1,600 to $9,400 per grant
Contact: John Briscoe

RHODE ISLAND

Rhode Island Advocacy Grants for the Developmentally Disabled
Office of Elementary and Secondary Education
22 Hayes Street
Providence, RI 02908
(401) 277-2031

Description: Grants to support developmentally disabled children and young people in achieving their maximum potential
$ Given: $1,050 to $8,700 per grant
Contact: Kenneth Mellor

SOUTH CAROLINA

South Carolina Advocacy Grants for the Developmentally Disabled
Office of Elementary and Secondary Education
1429 Senate St., Rm. 1008
Columbia, SC 29201
(803) 734-8488

Description: Grants to support developmentally disabled children and young people in achieving their maximum potential
$ Given: $1,020 to $9,300 per grant
Contact: Charlie G Williams

SOUTH DAKOTA

South Dakota Advocacy Grants for the Developmentally Disabled
Office of Elementary and Secondary Education
700 Governor's Drive
Pierre, SD 57501
(605) 773-3243

Description: Grants to support developmentally disabled children and young people in achieving their maximum potential
$ Given: $870 to $7,000 per grant
Contact: Henry Kosters

TENNESSEE

Tennessee Advocacy Grants for the Developmentally Disabled
Office of Elementary and Secondary Education
436 6th Avenue, North, Room 100
Nashville, TN 37219
(615) 741-2731

Description: Grants to support developmentally disabled children and young people in achieving their maximum potential
$ Given: $1,250 to $9,200 per grant
Contact: Brad Hurley

TEXAS

Texas Advocacy Grants for the Developmentally Disabled
Office of Elementary and Secondary Education
1701 North Congress Avenue, Room 3-104
Austin, TX 78701
(512) 463-9701

Description: Grants to support developmentally disabled children and young people in achieving their maximum potential
$ Given: $1,450 to $10,350 per grant
Contact: Lynn Moak

UTAH

Utah Advocacy Grants for the Developmentally Disabled
Office of Elementary and Secondary Education
250 East 500 South
Salt lake City, UT 84111
(801) 538-7500

Description: Grants to support developmentally disabled children and young people in achieving their maximum potential
$ Given: $1,100 to $7,500 per grant
Contact: Scott Cameron

VERMONT

Vermont Advocacy Grants for the Developmentally Disabled
Office of Elementary and Secondary Education
120 State Street
Montpelier, VT 05602
(802) 828-3135

Description: Grants to support developmentally disabled children and young people in achieving their maximum potential
$ Given: $1,200 to $8,900 per grant
Contact: Richard Mills

VIRGINIA

Virginia Advocacy Grants for the Developmentally Disabled
Office of Elementary and Secondary Education
101 North 14th Street
Richmond, VA 23216
(804) 224-2023

Description: Grants to support developmentally disabled children and young people in achieving their maximum potential
$ Given: $1,300 to $10,100 per grant
Contact: John Davis

WASHINGTON

Washington Advocacy Grants for the Developmentally Disabled
Office of Elementary and Secondary Education
Mail Stop FG 11
Olympia, WA 98504
(206) 753-6717

Description: Grants to support developmentally disabled children and young people in achieving their maximum potential
$ Given: $1,300 to $9,650 per grant
Contact: Doyle Winter

WEST VIRGINIA

West Virginia Advocacy Grants for the Developmentally Disabled
Office of Elementary and Secondary Education
1900 Washington Street, East,
Room B-358
Charleston, WV 25305
(304) 348-2681

Description: Grants to support developmentally disabled children and young people in achieving their maximum potential
$ Given: $950 to $9,200 per grant
Contact: Tom McNeel

WISCONSIN

Wisconsin Advocacy Grants for the Developmentally Disabled
Office of Elementary and Secondary Education
125 South Webster Street
Madison, WI 53707
(608) 266-1771

Description: Grants to support developmentally disabled children and young people in achieving their maximum potential
$ Given: $1,000 to $8,700 per grant
Contact: C. Richard Nelson

WYOMING

Wyoming Advocacy Grants for the Developmentally Disabled
Office of Elementary and Secondary Education
2300 Capitol Ave., 2nd Fl.
Cheyenne, WY 82002
(307) 777-7673

Description: Grants to support developmentally disabled children and young people in achieving their maximum potential
$ Given: $900 to $8,000 per grant
Contact: Lynn Simons

GRANTS FOR CHILDREN OF MIGRANT WORKERS

(Individuals may apply through state offices of education)

ALABAMA

Alabama Migrant Education Formula Grant
Office of Elementary and Secondary Education
State Office Bldg., Rm. 483
501 Dexter Avenue
Montgomery, AL 36130
(205) 261-5156

Description: Grants to address the educational needs of the children of migratory workers
$ Given: $1,500 to $8,000 per grant
Contact: Wayne Teague

ALASKA

Alaska Migrant Education Formula Grant
Office of Elementary and Secondary Education
801 West 10th Street,
P.O. Box F
Juneau, AK 99822
(907) 465-2800

Description: Grants to address the educational needs of the children of migratory workers
$ Given: $1,200 to $7,500 per grant
Contact: William Demmert

ARIZONA

Arizona Migrant Education Formula Grant
Office of Elementary and Secondary Education
1535 West Jefferson Street
Phoenix, AZ 85007
(602) 542-4361

Description: Grants to address the educational needs of the children of migratory workers
$ Given: $1,250 to $5,600 per grant
Contact: Diane Bishop

ARKANSAS

Arkansas Migrant Education Formula Grant
Office of Elementary and Secondary Education
4 Capitol Mall, Rm. 304-A
Little Rock, AR 72201
(501) 682-4204

Description: Grants to address the educational needs of the children of migratory workers
$ Given: $1,100 to $7,500 per grant
Contact: Ruth S Steele

CALIFORNIA

California Migrant Education Formula Grant
Office of Elementary and Secondary Education
721 Capitol Mall, Rm. 524
P.O. Box 944272
Sacramento, CA 94244
(916) 324-6874

Description: Grants to address the educational needs of the children of migratory workers
$ Given: $2,000 to $8,500 per grant
Contact: William D Dawson

COLORADO

Colorado Migrant Education Formula Grant
Office of Elementary and Secondary Education
201 East Colfax
Denver, CO 80203
(303) 866-6806

Description: Grants to address the educational needs of the children of migratory workers
$ Given: $2,100 to $6,700 per grant
Contact: Ray Kilmer

CONNECTICUT

Connecticut Migrant Education Formula Grant
Office of Elementary and Secondary Education
165 Capitol Avenue
P.O. Box 2219
Hartford, CT 06145
(203) 566-5061

Description: Grants to address the educational needs of the children of migratory workers
$ Given: Varies
Contact: Frank Altieri

DELAWARE

Delaware Migrant Education Formula Grant
Office of Elementary and Secondary Education
P.O. Box 1402
Dover, DE 19903
(302) 736-4601

Description: Grants to address the educational needs of the children of migratory workers
$ Given: $1,080 to $5,000 per grant
Contact: John J Ryan

FLORIDA

Florida Migrant Education Formula Grant
Office of Elementary and Secondary Education
The Capitol, Plaza Level 08
Tallahassee, FL 32399
(904) 448-0816

Description: Grants to address the educational needs of the children of migratory workers
$ Given: $2,250 to $8,000 per grant
Contact: Laurey Stryker

GEORGIA

Georgia Migrant Education Formula Grant
Office of Elementary and Secondary Education
205 Butler Street, SE
Atlanta, GA 30334
(404) 656-2800

Description: Grants to address the educational needs of the children of migratory workers
$ Given: $1,300 to $5,100 per grant
Contact: Werner Rogers

HAWAII

Hawaii Migrant Education Formula Grant
Office of Elementary and Secondary Education
1390 Miller Street,
P.O. Box 2360
Honolulu, HI 96804
(808) 548-5972

Description: Grants to address the educational needs of the children of migratory workers
$ Given: $850 to $5,000 per grant
Contact: Kengo Takata

IDAHO

Idaho Migrant Education Formula Grant
Office of Elementary and Secondary Education
650 West State St., Rm. 200
Boise, ID 83720
(208) 334-3301

Description: Grants to address the educational needs of the children of migratory workers
$ Given: $2,300 to $6,700 per grant
Contact: August M Hein

ILLINOIS

Illinois Migrant Education Formula Grant
Office of Elementary and Secondary Education
100 North First Street
Springfield, IL 62777
(217) 782-3371

Description: Grants to address the educational needs of the children of migratory workers
$ Given: $2,350 to $7,900 per grant
Contact: Dorothy Maggett

INDIANA

Indiana Migrant Education Formula Grant
Office of Elementary and Secondary Education
State House, Room 229
Indianapolis, IN 46204
(317) 269-9406

Description: Grants to address the educational needs of the children of migratory workers
$ Given: $1,990 to $6,200 per grant
Contact: Robert Dalton

IOWA

Iowa Migrant Education Formula Grant
Office of Elementary and Secondary Education
Grimes State Office Building
Des Moines, IA 50319
(515) 281-6731

Description: Grants to address the educational needs of the children of migratory workers
$ Given: $1,750 to $6,450 per grant
Contact: Sue Donielson

KANSAS

Kansas Migrant Education Formula Grant
Office of Elementary and Secondary Education
120 East 10th Street
Topeka, KS 66612
(913) 296-2303

Description: Grants to address the educational needs of the children of migratory workers
$ Given: $2,100 to $7,000 per grant
Contact: Sharon Freden

KENTUCKY

Kentucky Migrant Education Formula Grant
Office of Elementary and Secondary Education
Capitol Tower Plaza, 1st Fl.
Frankfort, KY 40601
(502) 564-4770

Description: Grants to address the educational needs of the children of migratory workers
$ Given: $2,375 to $6,150 per grant
Contact: Daniel Branham

LOUISIANA

Louisiana Migrant Education Formula Grant
Office of Elementary and Secondary Education
P.O. Box 94064
Baton Rouge, LA 70804
(504) 342-3602

Description: Grants to address the educational needs of the children of migratory workers
$ Given: $1,875 to $6,100 per grant
Contact: Wilmer S Cody

MAINE

Maine Migrant Education Formula Grant
Office of Elementary and Secondary Education
State House, Station 23
Augusta, ME 04333
(207) 289-5800

Description: Grants to address the educational needs of the children of migratory workers
$ Given: $1,500 to $5,500 per grant
Contact: Richard Card

MARYLAND

Maryland Migrant Education Formula Grant
Office of Elementary and Secondary Education
200 West Baltimore Street
Baltimore, MD 21201
(301) 333-2100

Description: Grants to address the educational needs of the children of migratory workers
$ Given: $2,300 to $6,500 per grant
Contact: Claud Kitchens

MASSACHUSETTS

Massachusetts Migrant Education Formula Grant
Office of Elementary and Secondary Education
1385 Hancock Street
Quincy, MA 02169
(617) 770-7200

Description: Grants to address the educational needs of the children of migratory workers
$ Given: $1,800 to $6,100 per grant
Contact: Fred Williams

MICHIGAN

Michigan Migrant Education Formula Grant
Office of Elementary and Secondary Education
P.O. Box 30008
Lansing, MI 48909
(517) 335-3537

Description: Grants to address the educational needs of the children of migratory workers
$ Given: $2,350 to $7,500 per grant
Contact: Douglas Roberts

MINNESOTA

Minnesota Migrant Education Formula Grant
Office of Elementary and Secondary Education
550 Cedar Street
St Paul, MN 55101
(612) 297-3115

Description: Grants to address the educational needs of the children of migratory workers
$ Given: $2,100 to $6,790 per grant
Contact: Robert Wedl

MISSISSIPPI

Mississippi Migrant Education Formula Grant
Office of Elementary and Secondary Education
550 High Street, Room 501
Jackson, MS 39205
(601) 359-3513

Description: Grants to address the educational needs of the children of migratory workers
$ Given: $1,350 to $5,600 per grant
Contact: Thomas Saterfiel

MISSOURI

Missouri Migrant Education Formula Grant
Office of Elementary and Secondary Education
205 Jefferson Street
Jefferson City, MO 65102
(314) 751-4446

Description: Grants to address the educational needs of the children of migratory workers
$ Given: $2,000 to $5,800 per grant
Contact: Robert E Bartman

MONTANA

Montana Migrant Education Formula Grant
Office of Elementary and Secondary Education
Capitol Building, Room 106
Helena, MT 59620
(406) 444-3654

Description: Grants to address the educational needs of the children of migratory workers
$ Given: $1,250 to $4,700 per grant
Contact: Jack Copps

NEBRASKA

Nebraska Migrant Education Formula Grant
Office of Elementary and Secondary Education
301 Centennial Mall, South
Lincoln, NE 68509
(402) 471-2465

Description: Grants to address the educational needs of the children of migratory workers
$ Given: $1,650 to $6,200 per grant
Contact: Larry Vontz

NEVADA

Nevada Migrant Education Formula Grant
Office of Elementary and Secondary Education
400 West King Street
Carson City, NV 89710
(702) 885-3104

Description: Grants to address the educational needs of the children of migratory workers
$ Given: $1,450 to $6,700 per grant
Contact: Marcia Bandera

NEW HAMPSHIRE

New Hampshire Migrant Education Formula Grant
Office of Elementary and Secondary Education
101 Pleasant Street
Concord, NH 03301
(603) 271-3145

Description: Grants to address the educational needs of the children of migratory workers
$ Given: $1,200 to $6,000 per grant
Contact: Charles Marston

NEW JERSEY

New Jersey Migrant Education Formula Grant
Office of Elementary and Secondary Education
225 West State Street
Trenton, NJ 08625
(609) 292-4450

Description: Grants to address the educational needs of the children of migratory workers
$ Given: $1,950 to $7,200 per grant
Contact: Saul Cooperman

NEW MEXICO

New Mexico Migrant Education Formula Grant
Office of Elementary and Secondary Education
300 Don Gaspar Avenue
Santa Fe, NM 87501
(505) 827-6635

Description: Grants to address the educational needs of the children of migratory workers
$ Given: $2,150 to $6,700 per grant
Contact: Alan D Morgan

NEW YORK

New York Migrant Education Formula Grant
Office of Elementary and Secondary Education
Education Building Annex
Albany, NY 12234
(518) 474-4688

Description: Grants to address the educational needs of the children of migratory workers
$ Given: $2,500 to $7,900 per grant
Contact: Lionel D Meno

NORTH CAROLINA

North Carolina Migrant Education Formula Grant
Office of Elementary and Secondary Education
116 West Edenton Street
Raleigh, NC 27603
(919) 733-3813

Description: Grants to address the educational needs of the children of migratory workers
$ Given: $1,850 to $7,200 per grant
Contact: Bobby Etheridge

NORTH DAKOTA

North Dakota Migrant Education Formula Grant
Office of Elementary and Secondary Education
State Capitol
Bismarck, ND 58505
(701) 224-2260

Description: Grants to address the educational needs of the children of migratory workers
$ Given: $900 to $6,900 per grant
Contact: Ron Stastney

OHIO

Ohio Migrant Education Formula Grant
Office of Elementary and Secondary Education
65 South Front Street, Room 808
Columbus, OH 43215
(614) 466-3708

Description: Grants to address the educational needs of the children of migratory workers
$ Given: $2,200 to $7,000 per grant
Contact: Irene G Bandy

OKLAHOMA

Oklahoma Migrant Education Formula Grant
Office of Elementary and Secondary Education
2500 North Lincoln Boulevard, Room 121
Oklahoma City, OK 73105
(405) 521-3301

Description: Grants to address the educational needs of the children of migratory workers
$ Given: $2,100 to $6,900 per grant
Contact: Judy Leach

OREGON

Oregon Migrant Education Formula Grant
Office of Elementary and Secondary Education
700 Pringle Parkway, SE
Salem, OR 97310
(503) 378-8518

Description: Grants to address the educational needs of the children of migratory workers
$ Given: $1,550 to $6,700 per grant
Contact: Ronald D Burge

PENNSYLVANIA

Pennsylvania Migrant Education Formula Grant
Office of Elementary and Secondary Education
333 Market Street, 10th Fl.
Harrisburg, PA 17126
(717) 787-5820

Description: Grants to address the educational needs of the children of migratory workers
$ Given: $2,100 to $6,500 per grant
Contact: Andrew Dinniman

RHODE ISLAND

Rhode Island Migrant Education Formula Grant
Office of Elementary and Secondary Education
22 Hayes Street
Providence, RI 02908
(401) 277-2031

Description: Grants to address the educational needs of the children of migratory workers
$ Given: $1,000 to $5,600 per grant
Contact: Kenneth P Mellor

SOUTH CAROLINA

South Carolina Migrant Education Formula Grant
Office of Elementary and Secondary Education
1429 Senate St., Rm. 1008
Columbia, SC 29201
(803) 734-8488

Description: Grants to address the educational needs of the children of migratory workers
$ Given: $1,300 to $6,900 per grant
Contact: Robert R Hill

SOUTH DAKOTA

South Dakota Migrant Education Formula Grant
Office of Elementary and Secondary Education
700 Governor's Drive
Pierre, SD 57501
(605) 773-3243

Description: Grants to address the educational needs of the children of migratory workers
$ Given: $850 to $5,500 per grant
Contact: Henry Kosters

TENNESSEE

Tennessee Migrant Education Formula Grant
Office of Elementary and Secondary Education
436 6th Avenue, North, Room 100
Nashville, TN 37219
(615) 741-2731

Description: Grants to address the educational needs of the children of migratory workers
$ Given: $1,500 to $7,100 per grant
Contact: Charles Smith

TEXAS

Texas Migrant Education Formula Grant
Office of Elementary and Secondary Education
1701 North Congress Ave., Room 3-104
Austin, TX 78701
(512) 463-9701

Description: Grants to address the educational needs of the children of migratory workers
$ Given: $2,900 to $8,800 per grant
Contact: Lynn M Moak

UTAH

Utah Migrant Education Formula Grant
Office of Elementary and Secondary Education
250 East 500 South
Salt lake City, UT 84111
(801) 538-7500

Description: Grants to address the educational needs of the children of migratory workers
$ Given: $1,300 to $5,700 per grant
Contact: Scott Cameron

VERMONT

Vermont Migrant Education Formula Grant
Office of Elementary and Secondary Education
120 State Street
Montpelier, VT 05602
(802) 828-3135

Description: Grants to address the educational needs of the children of migratory workers
$ Given: $950 to $5,400 per grant
Contact: Richard Mills

VIRGINIA

Virginia Migrant Education Formula Grant
Office of Elementary and Secondary Education
101 North 14th Street
Richmond, VA 23216
(804) 224-2023

Description: Grants to address the educational needs of the children of migratory workers
$ Given: $1,350 to $6,200 per grant
Contact: S. John Davis

WASHINGTON

Washington Migrant Education Formula Grant
Office of Elementary and Secondary Education
Mail Stop FG 11
Olympia, WA 98504
(206) 753-6717

Description: Grants to address the educational needs of the children of migratory workers
$ Given: $2,300 to $8,200 per grant
Contact: Doyle Winter

WEST VIRGINIA

West Virginia Migrant Education Formula Grant
Office of Elementary and Secondary Education
1900 Washington Street, East, Room B-358
Charleston, WV 25305
(304) 348-2681

Description: Grants to address the educational needs of the children of migratory workers
$ Given: $1,200 to $5,500 per grant
Contact: Tom McNeel

WISCONSIN

Wisconsin Migrant Education Formula Grant
Office of Elementary and Secondary Education
125 South Webster Street
Madison, WI 53707
(608) 266-1771

Description: Grants to address the educational needs of the children of migratory workers
$ Given: $2,100 to $6,900 per grant
Contact: C. Richard Nelson

WYOMING

Wyoming Migrant Education Formula Grant
Office of Elementary and Secondary Education
2300 Capitol Ave., 2nd Fl.
Cheyenne, WY 82002
(307) 777-7673

Description: Grants to address the educational needs of the children of migratory workers
$ Given: $1,000 to $5,000 per grant
Contact: Lynn Simons

FEDERAL PROGRAMS

Migrant Education High School Equivalency Program
Office of Migrant Education
Department of Education
400 Maryland Avenue, SW, Room 2141
Washington, DC 20202
(202) 732-4742

Description: Funding to assist the dropout children of migrant workers in obtaining their high school equivalency degrees
Amount Funded: $7,800,000
$ Given: Variable by need; 25 recipients per year
Contact: William Stormer

SPECIAL POPULATION FUNDING

FEDERAL FUNDING FOR MISCELLANEOUS POPULATIONS

Minority Science Improvement Grants
Division of Incentive Programs
Department of Education
400 Maryland Avenue, SW, Room 3030
Washington, DC 20202
(202) 732-4396

Description: Funding to allow minority high school students to have access to science and mathematics career education
Amount Funded: $5,633,000
$ Given: $1,000 to $1,800 per award
Who May Apply: Minority High School Students
Contact: Argelia Velez-Rodriquez

Native Hawaiian Gifted and Talented Student Grants
Department of Education
400 Maryland Avenue, SW
Washington, DC 20202
(202) 732-4342

Description: Funding to address the special needs of gifted and talented primary and secondary students in Hawaii
Amount Funded: $704,000
$ Given: Variable
Who May Apply: Individual
Contact: John Feigel

Promotion of the Humanities for Younger Scholars
Division of Fellowships and Seminars
National Endowment for the Humanities, Room 316
Washington, DC 20506
(202) 786-0463

Description: Funding to support summer-session humanities projects accomplished by advanced high school students
Amount Funded: $375,000
$ Given: $1,800 to $2,200 per award
Who May Apply: Qualified individuals
Contact: Director

Talent Search
Office of Student Services
Office of Elementary and Secondary Education
Department of Education
400 Maryland Avenue, SW, Room 3030
Washington, DC 20202
(202) 732-4804

Description: Funding program that identifies disadvantaged youth with potential for post-secondary education, encourages them to graduate, and familiarizes them with the varieties of financial aid available
Amount Funded: $147,000
$ Given: Variable
Who May Apply: Qualified high school students and dropouts
Contact: Goldia Hodgdon

Upward Bound
Office of Student Services
Office of Elementary and
Secondary Education
400 Maryland Avenue, SW,
Room 3030
Washington, DC 20202
(202) 732-4804

Description: Funding to generate secondary school success among low-income and potential first-generation college students
Amount Funded: $196,000
$ Given: $40 to $60 per month
Who May Apply: Qualified individuals
Contact: Goldia Hodgdon

Young Scholars Science and Mathematics Scholarships
Research and
Career Development
National Science Foundation, Room 630
1800 G Street, NW
Washington, DC 20550
(202) 357-7538

Description: Funding to identify and encourage secondary school students with high potential and ability in science and mathematics
Amount Funded: $7,000,000
$ Given: $2,000 to $3,500 per award
Who May Apply: Individuals
Contact: Dr. Elmina C. Johnson

Private School Financial Aid

This chapter covers the wide variety of support directly available from private schools across the United States. This support is offered to parents of every income levels and ranges widely. It can take the form of a child participating in a work-study program to help offset tuition costs, or it can be a straight full or partial scholarship based on ability or need.

As with other funding sources, the best approach is to call and speak with the person who is in charge of financial assistance to students. Ask for further information about qualifications, application procedures, and deadlines. Inquire as to where the school is in its assistance cycle; often, if you are not eligible for this year, you may be for next year. In addition, financial assistance officers may be able to refer you to other programs which can help you during the interim or can provide supplemental funding on an annual basis.

ALABAMA

The Altamont School
4801 Altamont Road
Birmingham, AL 35222
(205) 879-2006

Type of School: Co-ed college preparatory day school; grades 5-12
Tuition: $4,020 (grades 5 & 6); $4,668 (grade 7); $4,800 (grade 8); $5,064 (grades 9-12)
$ Given: $135,000 to 22% of student body
Additional Information: Students may contribute to tuition by working as clerical, library or lab assistants during the school year, or as maintenance assistants during the summer.

The Donoho School
2501 Henry Road
P.O. Box 2537
Anniston, AL 36202
(205) 237-5457

Type of School: Co-ed college preparatory day school; 500 students, pre-school through grade 12
Tuition: $2,200 to $3,020
$ Given: $75,000 to 105 students (21% of student body)
Contact: Roy T. Sheffield, President

Houston Academy
1001 Buena Vista Drive
Dothan, AL 36303
(205) 794-4106

Type of School: Co-ed preparatory day school; 480 students, pre-school through grade 12
Tuition: $910 to $3,335
$ Given: $50,000 to 105 students (21% of student body); subscribes to School Scholarship Service
Contact: Lydianne Merritt, Director of Administration

Indian Springs School
6000 Cahaba Valley Road
Helena, AL 35080
(205) 988-3350

Type of School: Co-ed college preparatory boarding and day school; 243 students, grades 8-12
Tuition: $10,975 (boarding); $6,100 (day)
$ Given: $359,788 to 66 students (27% of student body)
Contact: Charles H. Ellis, Director of Administration

UMS-Wright Preparatory School
65 N. Mobile Street
Mobile, AL 36607
(205) 479-6551

Type of School: Co-ed college preparatory day school; 1,000 students, pre-kindergarten through grade 12
Tuition: $1,600 to $3,600
$ Given: $90,000 to 180 students (18% of student body)
Contact: Tony W. Holland, Headmaster

ARIZONA

All Saints Episcopal Day School
6300 N. Central Avenue
Phoenix, AZ 85012
(602) 274–4866

Type of School: Co–ed; 350 students, kindergarten through grade 8
Tuition: $3,895 to $3,950
$ Given: $52,000 to 66 students (19% of student body)
Contact: Richard P. Ericksen, Headmaster

Green Fields Country Day School
6000 N. Camino dela Tierra
Tucson, AZ 85741
(602) 297–2288

Type of School: Co–ed; 200 students, grades 4–12
Tuition: $5,490
$ Given: $260,000 to 78 students (39% of student body)
Contact: Phineas Anderson, Headmaster

Judson School
P.O. Box 1569
Scottsdale, AZ 85252
(602) 948–7731

Type of School: Co–ed, kindergarten through grade 12; 248 boarding students; 142 day students
Tuition: $13,800 (boarding); $4,200 to $6,900 (day)
$ Given: Limited
Contact: Allan D. Hilton, Director of Administration

The Orme School
HC 63
Box 3040
Mayer, AZ 86333
(602) 632–7601

Type of School: Co–ed college preparatory boarding school, grades 9–12
Tuition: $13,500 (extras $1,500)
$ Given: $350,000 in scholarships and student loans based on citizenship, leadership and academic achievement
Contact: Peter Alford, Director of Administration

Verde Valley School
3511 Verde Valley School Rd.
Sedona, AZ 86336
(602) 284–2272

Type of School: Co–ed college preparatory boarding and day school; 78 students, grades 9–12
Tuition: $13,750 (boarding); $6,885 (day)
$ Given: $170,000 to 22 students (28% of student body)
Contact: Travis Ball, Jr., Director of Administration

ARKANSAS

Subiaco Academy
College Avenue
Subiaco, AR 72865
(501) 934–4291

Type of School: Roman Catholic college preparatory school for boys; grades 9–12
Tuition: $4,500 (boarding); $1,200 (day)
$ Given: Granted to approximately 30% of the student body; tuition grants total $110,000 with an additional $30,000 given through Self–Help Program
Contact: The Rev. Benno Schluterman, O.S.B.

CALIFORNIA

Brandeis Hillel Day School
655 Brotherhood Way
San Francisco, CA 94132
(415) 334–9841

Type of School: Co–ed day school (nondenominational Jewish environment); 378 students, grades K–8
Tuition: $4,250 to $4,650
$ Given: $225,000
Contact: Frederick S. Nathan, Director

Crossroads School for Arts and Sciences
Secondary Campus
1714 21st Street
Santa Monica, CA 90404
(213) 829–7391

Type of School: Co–ed day school; 653 students, grades 7–12
Tuition: $8,285 to $8,330
$ Given: $770,000 to 126 students (19% of student body)
Contact: Tom Nolan, Director of Administration

The Elliott–Pope Preparatory School
P.O. Box 338
Idyllwild, CA 92349
(714) 659–2191

Type of School: Co–ed college preparatory boarding and day school; 150 students, grades 7–12
Tuition: $15,200 (boarding); $7,650 (day)
$ Given: $305,000 to 50 students (33% of student body)
Contact: Jim Zuberbuhler, Director of Administration

The Harvard School
3700 Coldwater Canyon
North Hollywood, CA
91604–0037
(818) 980–6692

Type of School: College preparatory day school for boys; 828 students, grades 7–12
Tuition: $7,750
$ Given: $460,000 to 83 students (10% of student body)
Contact: Harry Salamandra, Dean of Students

The Idyllwild School of Music and the Arts
P.O. Box 38
52500 Temecula Road
Idyllwild, CA 92349
(714) 659–2171

Type of School: Co–ed boarding and day school; 100 students, grades 8–12
Tuition: $15,200 (boarding); $7,650 (day)
$ Given: $308,000 to 42 students (42% of student body)
Contact: Tom Brewley, Director of Administration

Menlo School
50 Valparaiso Avenue
Atherton, CA 94027
(415) 323–6141

Type of School: Co–ed day school; 444 students, grades 7–12 (boys) and 9–12 (girls)
Tuition: $7,390 to $8,980
$ Given: $410,000 to 115 students (26% of student body)
Contact: J. Anthony Paulus, Headmaster

San Francisco University High School
3065 Jackson Street
San Francisco, CA 95115
(415) 346–8400

Type of School: Co–ed; 380 students, grades 9–12
Tuition: $8,450
$ Given: $429,800 to 106 students (28% of student body)
Contact: Peter T. Esty, Headmaster

The Thacher School
Ojai, CA 93023
(805) 646–4377

Type of School: Co–ed boarding school; 228 students, grades 9–12
Tuition: $15,350
$ Given: $428,000 to 48 students (21% of student body)
Contact: Joy Sawyer Mulligan, Director of Administration

Webb Schools
1175 W. Base Line Road
Claremont, CA 91711
(714) 626–3587

Type of School: Boarding and day school for boys, grades 9–12; Vivian Webb boarding and day school for girls, grades 9–12; 361 students
Tuition: $16,300 (boarding); $9,000 (day)
$ Given: $587,550 to 54 students (15% of student body)
Contact: Nigel Taplin, Director of Administration

COLORADO

Alexander Dawson School
4801 N. 107th Street
Lafayette, CO 80026
(303) 665–6679

Type of School: Co–ed college preparatory boarding and day school; 125 students, grades 6–12
Tuition: $11,400 (boarding); $6,400 (day)
$ Given: $300,000 to 50 students (40% of student body)
Contact: Lynn Israel, Director of Administration

Aspen Country Day School
P.O. Box 2466
1038 Castle Creek Road
Aspen, CO 81612
(303) 925-1909

Type of School: Co–ed day school; 150 students, pre–kindergarten through grade 12
Tuition: $4,925 to $7,500
$ Given: $100,000 to 39 students (26% of student body)
Contact: Ashley J. Owen, Head of School

Colorado Academy
3800 S. Pierre Street
Denver, CO 80235
(303) 986–1501

Type of School: Co–ed day school; 600 students, pre–school through grade 12
Tuition: $4,250 to $7,300
$ Given: $375,000 to 156 students (26% of student body)
Contact: Frank Wallace, Headmaster

Colorado Rocky Mountain School
Box N, 1493 Road 106
Carbondale, CO 81623
(303) 963–2562

Type of School: Co–ed college preparatory boarding and day school; 148 students, grades 9–12
Tuition: $14,850 (boarding); $8,175 (day)
$ Given: $375,000 to 41 students (28% of student body)

Fountain Valley School
Colorado Springs, CO
80911
(719) 390–7035

Type of School: Co–ed college preparatory boarding and day school; 222 students, grades 9–12
Tuition: $14,000 (boarding); $8,000 (day)
$ Given: $460,000 to 55 students (25% of student body)
Contact: Nancy L. Harley, Director of Administration

• • • • • • • • • • • • • • • • • • •

Graland Country Day School
30 Birch Street
Denver, CO 80220
(303) 399–0390

Type of School: Co–ed; 565 students, kindergarten through grade 9
Tuition: $4,800 to $6,200
$ Given: $317,000 to 141 students (25% of student body)
Contact: Larry W. Doherty, Headmaster

Kent Denver School
4000 E. Quincy Avenue
Englewood, CO 80110
(303) 770–7660

Type of School: Co–ed day school; 500 students, grades 6–12
Tuition: $7,300
$ Given: $425,000 to 135 students (27% of student body)
Contact: Thomas Kaesemeyer, Headmaster

St. Anne's Episcopal School
2701 S. York Street
Denver, CO 80210
(303) 756–9481

Type of School: Co–ed Montessori day school; 402 students, pre–kindergarten through grade 8
Tuition: $3,139 to $5,086
$ Given: $180,000 to 105 students (26% of student body)
Contact: John Comfort, Headmaster

CONNECTICUT

Avon Old Farms School
Avon, CT 06001
(203) 673–3201

Type of School: Boys' boarding and day school; 376 students, grades 9–12
Tuition: $14,900 (boarding); $8,700 (day)
$ Given: $540,000 to 79 students (21% of student body)
Contact: Frank G. Leavitt, Director of Administration

Brunswick School
100 Maher Avenue
Greenwich, CT 06830
(203) 869–0601

Type of School: College preparatory day school for boys; 550 students, pre–kindergarten through grade 12
Tuition: $4,500 to $9,750
$ Given: $415,000 to 143 students (26% of student body)
Contact: Duncan Edwards III, Headmaster

Canterbury School
Aspetuck Avenue
New Milford, CT 06776
(203) 355–3103

Type of School: Co–ed boarding and day school; 281 students, grades 9–12
Tuition: $15,500 (boarding); $9,600 (day)
$ Given: $800,000 to 101 students (36% of student body)
Contact: Patrick M. Finn, Director of Administration

Cheshire Academy
10 Main Street
Cheshire, CT 06410
(203) 272–5396

Type of School: Co–ed boarding and day school; 242 students, grades 6–12
Tuition: $15,675 (boarding); $7,975 to $8,975 (day)
$ Given: $385,000 to 56 students (23% of student body)
Contact: Patricia H. Monahan, Director of Administration

Choate Rosemary Hall
333 Christian Street
Wallingford, CT 06492
(203) 269–7722

Type of School: Co–ed boarding and day school; 982 students, grades 9–12
Tuition: $14,800 (boarding); $10,250 (day)
$ Given: $2,500,000 to 344 students (35% of student body)
Contact: Charles F. Dey, Principal

The Hotchkiss School
Lakeville, CT 06039
(203) 435–2591

Type of School: Co–ed boarding and day school; 523 students, grades 9–12
Tuition: $14,100 (boarding); $9,700 (day)
$ Given: $1,152,000 to 139 students (26.5% of student body)
Contact: Dr. Parnell P. Hagerman, Director of Administration

Kent School
Kent, CT 06757
(203) 927–3501

Type of School: Co–ed boarding and day school; 556 students, grades 9–12
Tuition: $15,200 (boarding); $10,500 (day)
$ Given: $850,000 to 150 students (27% of student body)
Contact: M. Willard Lampe II, Director of Administration

The Loomis Chaffee School
Windsor, CT 06095
(203) 688–4934

Type of School: Co–ed boarding and day school; 700 students, grades 9–12
Tuition: $15,100 (boarding); $10,250 (day)
$ Given: $1,200,000 to 175 students (25% of student body)
Contact: Drew J. Casertano, Director of Administration

Suffield Academy
High Street
Suffield, CT 06078
(203) 688–7315

Type of School: Co–ed boarding and day school; 315 students, grades 9–12
Tuition: $14,800 (boarding); $9,100 (day)
$ Given: $687,770 to 104 students (33% of student body)
Contact: Terence J. Ullram, Director of Administration

DELAWARE

Archmere Academy
P.O. Box 130
3600 Philadelphia Pike
Claymont, DE 19703
(302) 798–6632

Type of School: Co–ed Roman Catholic college preparatory day school; 544 students, grades 9–12
Tuition: $6,640
$ Given: $320,000 to 131 students (24% of student body)
Contact: The Rev. Joseph A. McLaughlin

St. Andrew's School
Middletown, DE 19709
(302) 834–5350

Type of School: Co–ed college preparatory day school; 238 students, grades 9–12
Tuition: $13,500
$ Given: $904,650 to 98 students (41% of student body)
Contact: John M. Niles, Director of Administration

St. Mark's High School
Pike Creek Road
Wilmington, DE 19808
(302) 738–3300

Type of School: Co–ed Roman Catholic day school; 1,303 students, grades 9–12
Tuition: $2,520
$ Given: $100,000 to 235 students (18% of student body)
Contact: Ronald R. Russo, Principal

Sanford School
Lancaster Pike
Hockessin, DE 19707
(302) 239–5263

Type of School: Co–ed day school; 460 students, pre–kindergarten through grade 12
Tuition: $4,085 to $7,545
$ Given: $225,000 to 106 students (23% of student body)
Contact: Gordon T. Schofield, Headmaster

The Tatnall School
1501 Barley Mill Road
Wilmington, DE 19807
(302) 998–2292

Type of School: Co–ed college preparatory day school; 710 students, nursery through grade 12
Tuition: $3,275 to $7,55
$ Given: $445,600 to 192 students (27% of student bo
Contact: William E. Ricketson, Jr., Headmaster

Tower Hill School
2813 West 17th Street
Wilmington, DE 19806
(302) 575–0550

Type of School: Co–ed day school; 668 students, grades K–12
Tuition: $3,540 to $8,100
$ Given: $575,000 to 200 students (30% of student body)

Wilmington Friends School
101 School Road
Alapocas
Wilmington, DE 19803
(302) 575–1130

Type of School: Co–ed Quaker day school; 700 students, pre–kindergarten through grade 12
Tuition: $4,000 to $7,600
$ Given: $566,600 to 203 students (29% of student body)
Contact: Dulany O. Bennett, Head of School

DISTRICT OF COLUMBIA

Beauvoir, The National Cathedral Elementary School
3500 Woodley Road, NW
Washington, DC 20016
(202) 537–6492

Type of School: Co–ed day school; 356 students, nursery through grade 3
Tuition: $5,665 to $6,170
$ Given: $160,000 to 82 students (23% of student body)
Contact: Mrs. William F. Moreland, Headmistress

Georgetown Day School Lower/Middle School
4530 MacArthur Blvd., NW
Washington, DC 20007
(202) 333–7727

Type of School: Co–ed college preparatory school; 921 students, pre–kindergarten through grade 12
Tuition: $7,632 to $8,808
$ Given: $632,500 to 212 students (23% of student body)
Contact: Gladys M. Stern, Director

High School
4200 Davenport Street, NW
Washington, DC 20016
(202) 966–2666

Type of School: Co–ed college preparatory school; 921 students, pre–kindergarten through grade 12
Tuition: $7,632 to $8,808
$ Given: $632,500 to 212 students (23% of student body)
Contact: Gladys M. Stern, Director

National Cathedral School
Mount St. Alban
Washington, DC 20016
(202) 537–6374

Type of School: Girls' Episcopal college preparatory day school; 540 students, grades 4–12
Tuition: $9,380
$ Given: $422,000 to 124 students (23% of student body)
Contact: Agnes Cochran Underwood, Headmaster

St. Albans School
Mount St. Alban
Washington, DC 20016
(202) 537–6400

Type of School: Boys' Episcopal college preparatory day school; 543 students, grades 4–12
Tuition: $13,800 (boarding); $8,925 (day)
$ Given: $575,000 to 114 students (21% of student body)
Contact: Henri Billey, Dean of Students

St. Patrick's Episcopal Day School
4700 Whitehaven Parkway, NW
Washington, DC 20007
(202) 342–2800

Type of School: Co–ed day school; 380 students, nursery through grade 6
Tuition: $4,400 to $6,930
$ Given: $192,500 to 91 students (24% of student body)
Contact: Robert Ross Peterson, Head of School

The Sidewell Friends School
3825 Wisconsin Avenue, NW
Washington, DC 20016
(202) 537–8100

Type of School: Co–ed Quaker college preparatory day school; 1,000 students, pre–kindergarten through grade 12
Tuition: $6,960 to $8,895
$ Given: $900,000 to 260 students (26% of student body)
Contact: Earl G. Harrison, Jr., Headmaster

Washington International School
3100 Macomb Street, NW
Washington, DC 20008
(202) 364–1800

Type of School: Co–ed day school; 614 students, nursery through grade 12
Tuition: $2,700 to $7,900
$ Given: $415,000 to 172 students (28% of student body)
Contact: Dexter Lewis, Headmaster

FLORIDA

The Bolles School
7400 San Jose Boulevard
Jacksonville, FL 32217–3499
(904) 733–9292

Type of School: Co–ed boarding school for boys; 1,140 students, kindergarten through grade 12
Tuition: $9,050 to $10,550 (boarding); $2,300 to $5,550 (day)
$ Given: $529,882 to 251 students (22% of student body)
Contact: Quinn R. Barton, Jr., Director of Administration

The Canterbury School
8141 College Parkway
Fort Myers, FL 33919
(813) 481–4323

Type of School: Co–ed day school; 350 students, junior kindergarten through grade 12
Tuition: $2,350 to $4,850
$ Given: $250,000 to 123 students (35% of student body)
Contact: Frank L. Romano, Headmaster

Carrollton School of the Sacred Heart
3747 Main Highway
Miami, FL 33133
(305) 446–5673

Type of School: Roman Catholic girls' day school; 490 students, pre–kindergarten through grade 12
Tuition: $4,400 to $6,200
$ Given: $200,000 to 113 students (23% of student body)
Contact: Sr. Ann Taylor, Headmistress

Miami Country Day School
P.O. Box 380608
601 N.E. 107th Street
Miami, FL 33238–0608
(305) 759–2843

Type of School: Co–ed, junior kindergarten through grade 12
Tuition: $3,900 to $6,750
$ Given: $361,550
Contact: William J. Creeden, Headmaster

Ransom Everglades School
Coconut Grove, FL 33133
(305) 460–8800

Type of School: Co–ed; 695 students, grades 7–12
Tuition: $7,450
$ Given: $385,000 to 153 students (22% of student body)
Contact: Frank J. Hogan III, Headmaster

St. Andrew's School of Boca Raton
Boca Raton, FL 33434
(407) 483–8900

Type of School: Co–ed boarding and day school; 574 students, grades 6–12
Tuition: $13,000 (boarding); $5,800 to $7,100 (day)
$ Given: $400,000 to 86 students (15% of student body)
Contact: Edward B. Wilson, Director of Administration

Tampa Preparatory School
625 North Boulevard
Tampa, FL 33606
(813) 251–8481

Type of School: Co–ed day school; 295 students, grades 9–12
Tuition: $5,900
$ Given: $125,000 to 65 students (22% of student body)

GEORGIA

Athens Academy
P.O. Box 6548
1281 Spartan Lane
Athens, GA 30604
(404) 549–9225

Type of School: Co–ed day school; 634 students, pre–kindergarten through grade 12
Tuition: $1,530 to $3,849
$ Given: $232,715 to 184 students (29% of student body)
Contact: J. Roberts Chambers, Headmaster

Brookstone School
440 Bradley Park Drive
Columbus, GA 31995
(404) 324–1392

Type of School: Co–ed day school; 4–year kindergarten through grade 12
Tuition: $2,600 to $4,400
$ Given: $179,000
Contact: Charles J. Camiskey, Headmaster

Darlington School
Rome, GA 30161
(404) 235–6051

Type of School: Co–ed boarding and day school; 845 students, grades 9 through post–graduate (boarding) and pre–kindergarten through post–graduate (day)
Tuition: $11,700 (boarding); $3,700 to $4,800 (day)
$ Given: $500,000 to 125 students (15% of student body)
Contact: Lisa B. Schlenk, Administrator

The Lovett School
4075 Paces Ferry Road, NW
Atlanta, GA 30327
(404) 262–3032

Type of School: Co–ed; 1,460 students, 4-year kindergarten through grade 12
Tuition: $3,490 to $6,610
$ Given: $400,000 to 292 students (20% of student body)
Contact: Fontaine Y. Draper, Administrator

Marist School
3790 Ashford–Dunwoody Rd.
Atlanta, GA 30319
(404) 457–7201

Type of School: Roman Catholic co–ed day school; 944 students, grades 7–12
Tuition: $4,520
$ Given: $175,000 to 179 students (19% of student body)
Contact: The Rev. Francis J. Kissel, Director of Administration

Pace Academy
966 W. Paces Ferry Road, NW
Atlanta, GA 30327
(404) 262–1345

Type of School: Co–ed day school; 765 students, pre–first through grade 12
Tuition: $4,100 to $6,450
$ Given: $250,000 to 90 students (12% of student body)
Contact: Dr. George Mengert, Administrator

The Westminister Schools
1424 W. Paces Ferry Road, NW
Atlanta, GA 30327
(404) 355–8673

Type of School: Co–ed day school; 1,685 students, pre–first through grade 12
Tuition: $3,960 to $6,785
$ Given: $604,000 to 371 students (22% of student body)
Contact: Robert Sims, Director of Administration

HAWAII

Assets School
P.O. Box 106
Pearl Harbor, HI 96860
(808) 423–1356

Type of School: Co–ed day school for gifted and learning disabled; 250 students, kindergarten through grade 8
Tuition: $4,900
$ Given: $40,000 to $90,000 to 50 students (20% of student body)
Contact: Barrett B. McCandless, Director

The Hawaii Preparatory Academy
Kamuela, HI 96743
(808) 885–7321

Type of School: Co–ed boarding and day school; 680 students, grades 6–12 (boarding), and kindergarten through grade 12 (day)
Tuition: $4,600 to $12,300
$ Given: $187,000 to 72 students (11% of student body)
Contact: Todd Anderson, Director of Administration

Iolani School
563 Kamoku Street
Honolulu, HI 96826
(808) 949–5355

Type of School: Co–ed day school; 1,748 students, kindergarten through grade 12
Tuition: $4,800
$ Given: $556,000 to 384 students (22% of student body)
Contact: The Rev. David P. Coon, Headmaster

La Pietra–Hawaii School for Girls
2933 Poni Moi Road
Honolulu, HI 96815
(808) 922–2744

Type of School: Day school for girls; 150 students, grades 6–12
Tuition: $4,500 to $4,800
$ Given: $135,000 to 51 students (34% of student body)
Contact: Joseph H. Pynchon, Headmaster

Mid–Pacific Institute
2445 Kaala Street
Honolulu, HI 96822
(808) 973–5000

Type of School: Co–ed boarding (91 students, grades 9–12) and day (1019 students, grades 7–12) school
Tuition: $4,825 (day); $7,725 (boarding)
$ Given: $140,000 to 189 students (17% of student body)

Punahou School
1601 Punahou Street
Honolulu, HI 96822
(808) 944-5711

Type of School: Co–ed day school; 3,700 students, kindergarten through grade 12
Tuition: $4,600 to $5,110
$ Given: $500,000 to 666 students (18% of student body)
Contact: Roderick F. McPhee, President

IDAHO

The Community School
P.O. Box 2118
Ketchum, ID 83340
(208) 622–3955

Type of School: Co–ed day school; 220 students, kindergarten through grade 12
Tuition: $5,950
$ Given: $104,000 to 51 students (23% of student body)
Contact: Jon Maksik, Headmaster

ILLINOIS

Chicago Junior School
1600 Dundee Avenue
Elgin, IL 60120
(708) 888–7910

Type of School: Co–ed day and boarding school; 200 students, grades 1–8 (boarding), and pre–school through grade 8 (day)
Tuition: $10,740 to $12,520 (boarding); $4,480 to $5,390 (day)
$ Given: $250,000 to 60 students (30% of student body)

Elgin Academy
350 Park Street
Elgin, IL 60120
(312) 695–0300

Type of School: Co–ed day school; 280 students, kindergarten through grade 12
Tuition: $3,950 to $7,250
$ Given: $240,000 to 84 students (30% of student body)
Contact: Selden S. Edwards, Headmaster

Francis W. Parker School
330 W. Webster Avenue
Chicago, IL 60614
(312) 549–0172

Type of School: Co–ed day school; 777 students, junior kindergarten through grade 12
Tuition: $6,000 to $8,400
$ Given: $820,000 to 233 students (30% of student body)
Contact: John P. Cotton, Principal

Keith Country Day School
1 Jacoby Place
Rockford, IL 61107
(815) 399–8823

Type of School: Co–ed day school; 316 students, grades K–12
Tuition: $2,025 to $5,200
$ Given: $195,000 to 101 students (32% of student body)

Lake Forest Academy
1500 W. Kennedy Road
Lake Forest, IL 60045
(708) 615–3267

Type of School: Co–ed boarding and day school; 275 students, grades 9–12
Tuition: $13,500 (boarding); $8,800 (day)
$ Given: $455,000 to 66 students (24% of student body)
Contact: Jacqueline R. Lainbach, Director of Administration

Lake Forest Country Day School
145 South Green Bay Road
Lake Forest, IL 60045
(708) 234–2350

Type of School: Co–ed day school; 431 students, 3–year pre–school through grade 9
Tuition: $1,950 to $7,350
$ Given: $232,000 to 116 students (27% of student body)
Contact: James L. Marks III, Headmaster

Roycemore School
640 Lincoln Street
Evanston, IL 60201
(312) 866–6055

Type of School: Co–ed day school; 220 students, junior kindergarten through grade 12
Tuition: $4,050 to $8,150
$ Given: $280,000 to 79 students (36% of student body)
Contact: Joseph A. Becker, Headmaster

The University of Chicago
Laboratory Schools
1362 E. 59th Street
Chicago, IL 60637
(312) 702–9450

Type of School: Four (4) co–ed day schools; 1,450 students, 3-year-olds' nursery through grade 12
Tuition: $3,400 to $6,700
$ Given: $240,000 to 261 students (18% of student body)
Contact: Alice Haskell, Director of Administration

INDIANA

Cathedral High School
5225 East 56th Street
Indianapolis, IN 46225
(317) 542–1481

Type of School: Roman Catholic co–ed day school; 629 students, grades 9–12
Tuition: $2,950
$ Given: $250,000 to 176 students (28% of student body)
Contact: Julian T. Peebles, President

Culver Military Academy
Culver Girls Academy
Culver, IN 46511
(219) 842–8200

Type of School: College preparatory boarding and day school for boys and girls; 676 students, grades 9–12
Tuition: $13,550 (boarding); $8,800 (day)
$ Given: $1,966,250 plus $28,000 in student loans annually to over 30% of student body
Contact: Richard A. Edwards, Director of Administration

Evansville Day School
3400 N. Green River Road
Evansville, IN 47715
(812) 476–3039

Type of School: Co–ed preparatory school; 375 students, pre–kindergarten through grade 12
Tuition: $2,400 to $5,000
$ Given: $390,000 to 161 students (43% of student body)
Contact: Lee R. Hensley, Headmaster

Howe Military School
Howe, IN 46746
(219) 562–2131

Type of School: Military boarding school for boys and girls; 225 students, grades 5–12
Tuition: $11,300
$ Given: $207,000 to 75 cadets (33% of student body)
Contact: Glenn R. Cox, Director of Administration

The Orchard Country Day School
615 West 63rd Street
Indianapolis, IN 46260
(317) 251–9253

Type of School: Co–ed day school; 542 students, nursery through grade 8
Tuition: $1,500 to $4,400
$ Given: $174,140
Contact: Charles F. Clark, Headmaster

Park Tudor School
7200 N. College Avenue
P.O. Box 40488
Indianapolis, IN 46240–0488
(317) 254–2700

Type of School: Co–ed college preparatory day school; 712 students, pre–kindergarten through grade 12
Tuition: $3,000 to $5,780
$ Given: 1 student in 6 receives funding; average grant equals half of tuition
Contact: C. Davies Reed, Director of Administration

The Stanley Clark School
3123 Miami
South Bend, IN 46614–2098
(219) 291–4200

Type of School: Co–ed private elementary day school; 355 students, kindergarten through grade 8
Tuition: $2,270 to $4,910
$ Given: $135,945 to 92 students (26% of student body)
Contact: Robert G. Douglass, Headmaster

IOWA

Scattergood Friends School
P.O. Box 32, Rural Route 1
West Branch, IA 52358
(319) 643–5636

Type of School: Quaker college preparatory boarding and day school; 65 students, grades 9–12
Tuition: $7,700
$ Given: $100,000 to 23 students (35% of student body)
Contact: Christopher Hinshaw, Director

KANSAS

Academy of Mount Saint Scholastica
1034 Green Street
Atchison, KS 66002
(913) 367–1334

Type of School: Girls' day and boarding school; 140 students, grades 9–12
Tuition: $6,100 (boarding); $1,200 (day)
$ Given: $25,000 to 28 students (20% of student body)
Contact: Sr. Dorothy Wolters, O.S.B., Principal

St. John's Military School
Box 827
End of North Santa Fe
Salina, KS 67402–0827
(913) 823–7231

Type of School: Boys' boarding school; 200 students, grades 5–12
Tuition: $9,545 (extras $1,500)
$ Given: $35,000 to 34 students (17% of student body)
Contact: Keith G. Ducker, President

Wichita Collegiate School
9115 E. Thirteenth Street
Wichita, KS 67206
(316) 684–0263

Type of School: Co–ed day school; 738 students, pre–school through grade 12
Tuition: $4,100 to $4,400
$ Given: $185,000 to 155 students (21% of student body)
Contact: Leonard Kupersmith, Headmaster

KENTUCKY

Kentucky Country Day School
4100 Springdale Road
Louisville, KY 40241
(502) 423–0440

Type of School: Co–ed day school; 619 students, kindergarten through grade 12
Tuition: $2,865 to $5,940
$ Given: $320,000 to 167 students (27% of student body)
Contact: Douglas C. Eveleth, Headmaster

The Lexington School
1050 Allen Road
Lexington, KY 40504
(606) 278–0501

Type of School: Co–ed day school; 451 students, 3-year-olds' nursery through grade 9
Tuition: $2,220 to $5,760
$ Given: $100,000 to 95 students (21% of student body)
Contact: Carolyn D. Blackburn, Director of Administration

Louisville Collegiate School
2427 Glenmary Avenue
Louisville, KY 40204
(502) 451–5330

Type of School: Co–ed college preparatory day school, kindergarten through grade 12
Tuition: $2,940 $5,665
$ Given: $170,000
Contact: Arnold E. Holtberg, Head of School

St. Francis School
11000 West Highway #42
Goshen, KY 40026
(502) 228–1197

Type of School: Co–ed day school; 233 students, kindergarten through grade 8
Tuition: $3,275 to $5,625
$ Given: $136,000 to 65 students (28% of student body)
Contact: J. Robertson MacColl IV, Headmaster

Sayre School
194 N. Limestone Avenue
Lexington, KY 40507
(606) 254–1361

Type of School: Co–ed; 450 students, pre–kindergarten through grade 12
Tuition: $2,400 to $4,700
$ Given: $66,500 to 86 students (19% of student body)

University Heights Academy
P.O. Box 1070
1300 Academy Drive
Hopkinsville, KY 42240
(502) 886–0254

Type of School: Co–ed day and five–day boarding school; 195 students, pre–kindergarten through grade 12
Tuition: $675 to $3,350
$ Given: $80,000 to 68 students (35% of student body)
Contact: Marvin D. Denison, Headmaster

LOUISIANA

Episcopal High School
3200 Woodland Ridge Blvd.
Baton Rouge, LA 70816
(504) 293–3180

Type of School: Co–ed college preparatory day school; 768 students, grades 4–12
Tuition: $2,250 to $5,100
$ Given: $374,373 to 215 students (28% of student body)
Contact: Paul B. Hancock, Headmaster

The Louise S. McGehee School
2343 Prytania Street
New Orleans, LA 70130
(504) 561–1224

Type of School: Girls' preparatory day school; 272 students, pre–kindergarten through grade 12
Tuition: $2,475 to $6,275
$ Given: Financial aid available
Contact: Margaret Wagner, Headmistress

Metairie Park Country Day School
300 Park Road
Metairie, LA 70005
(504) 837–5204

Type of School: Co–ed college preparatory school; 686 students, kindergarten through grade 12
Tuition: $3,270 to $5,975
$ Given: $182,250 to 144 students (21% of student body)
Contact: Edward Cosby Becker, Headmaster

St. Andrew's Episcopal School
8012 Oak Street
New Orleans, LA 70118
(504) 861–3743

Type of School: Co–ed day school; 155 students, pre–kindergarten through grade 6
Tuition: $2,500 to $3,400
$ Given: $70,000 to 47 students (30% of student body)
Contact: Gary J. Mannina, Headmaster

St. Martin's Episcopal School
5309 Airline Highway
Metairie, LA 70003
(504) 733–0353

Type of School: Co–ed day school; 862 students, pre–kindergarten through grade 12
Tuition: $2,600 to $6,030
$ Given: $450,000 to 233 students (27% of student body)
Contact: Donald S. Schwartz, Headmaster

Southfield School
1100 Southfield Road
Shreveport, LA 71106
(318) 868–5375

Type of School: College preparatory day school; 320 students, pre–school through grade 12
Tuition: $1,200 to $4,100
$ Given: $188,000 to 118 students (37% of student body)
Contact: Marion K. Marks, Headmaster

Trinity Episcopal School
2111 Chestnut Street
New Orleans, LA 70130
(504) 525–8661

Type of School: Co–ed day school; 400 students, pre–kindergarten through grade 8
Tuition: $2,800 to $5,640
$ Given: $100,000 to 84 students (21% of student body)
Contact: Edward P. Cavin, Headmaster

MAINE

Berwick Academy
31 Academy Street
South Berwick, ME 03908
(207) 384–2164

Type of School: Co–ed; 246 students, grades 1–12
Tuition: $6,500 to $7,500
$ Given: $115,000 to 54 students (22% of student body)
Contact: Richard "Hap" Ridgway, Headmaster

Carrabassett Valley Academy
Carrabassett Valley, ME 04947
(207) 237–2250

Type of School: Co–ed; 60 students, grades 7 through post–graduate
Tuition: $13,000 (boarding); $7,500 (day)
$ Given: $100,000 to 19 students (31% of student body)
Contact: John C. Ritzo, Headmaster

Fryeburg Academy
Fryeburg, ME 04037
(207) 935–2001

Type of School: Co–ed boarding and day school; 526 students, grades 9–12
Tuition: $11,600 (boarding); $5,800 (day)
$ Given: $120,000 to 95 students (18% of student body)
Contact: Harry G. True, Director of Administration

Hebron Academy
Hebron, ME 04238
(207) 966–2100

Type of School: Co–ed boarding and day school; 225 students, grades 9–12
Tuition: $15,900 (boarding); $8,900 (day)
$ Given: $420,000 to 86 students (38% of student body)
Contact: Kenneth W. Michelsen, Director of Administration

Kents Hill School
Kents Hill, ME 04349
(207) 685–4914

Type of School: Co–ed boarding and day school; 300 students, grades 9–12
Tuition: $14,900 (boarding); $6,000 (day)
$ Given: $225,000 to 66 students (22% of student body)
Contact: Mary E. Marble, Administrator

Maine Central Institute
Pittsfield, ME 04967
(207) 487–3355

Type of School: Co–ed boarding and day school; 496 students, grades 9–12
Tuition: $12,500 (boarding); $5,200 (day)
$ Given: $125,000 to 89 students (18% of student body)
Contact: Janet Washburn, Director of Administration

MARYLAND

The Bryn Mawr School
109 W. Melrose Avenue
Baltimore, MD 21210
(301) 323–8800

Type of School: Girls' day school; 653 students, pre–first through grade 12
Tuition: $6,300 to $7,550
$ Given: $460,300 to 163 students (25% of student body)
Contact: Barbara L. Chase, Headmaster

Friends School of Baltimore
5114 N. Charles Street
Baltimore, MD 21210
(301) 435–2800

Type of School: Quaker co–ed; 902 students, pre–primary through grade 12
Tuition: $5,700 to $7,250
$ Given: $665,000 to 234 students (26% of student body)
Contact: W. Byron Forbush, Headmaster

Garrison Forest School
Garrison, MD 21055
(301) 363–1500

Type of School: Girls' boarding and day school; 499 students, pre–school through grade 12
Tuition: $15,100 (boarding); $950 to $8,200 (day)
$ Given: $412,000 to 125 students (25% of student body), plus $120,000 in low–interest long-term loans
Contact: Nancy–Bets Hay, Director of Administration

Georgetown Preparatory School
10900 Rockville Pike
Rockville, MD 20852–3299
(301) 493–5000

Type of School: Boys' Roman Catholic boarding and day school; 399 students, grades 9–12
Tuition: $16,000 (boarding); $8,500 (day)
$ Given: $350,000 to 63 students (16% of student body)
Contact: Michael Horsey, Director of Administration

Gilman School
5407 Roland Avenue
Baltimore, MD 21210
(301) 323–3800

Type of School: Boys' day school, pre–first through grade 12
Tuition: $6,400– to $7,500
$ Given: $581,350
Contact: Redmond C.S. Finney, Headmaster

The Holton–Arms School
7303 River Road
Bethesda, MD 20817
(301) 365–5300

Type of School: Girls' day school; 615 students, grades 3–12
Tuition: $8,550
$ Given: $371,500
Contact: Charles P. Lord, Headmaster

McDonogh School
McDonogh, MD 21117–0380
(301) 363–0600

Type of School: Co–ed day and five-day boarding school; 1,162 students, grades 9–12 (boarding), and pre–first through grade 12 (day)
Tuition: $10,000 (boarding); $6,500 to $7,500 (day)
$ Given: $725,000 to 133 students (11% of student body)
Contact: Dawn Marie Cunnion, Director of Administration

The Park School of Baltimore
Old Court Road
Brooklandville, MD 21022
(301) 825–2351

Type of School: Co–ed; 691 students, nursery through grade 12
Tuition: $6,060 to $8,060
$ Given: $584,730 to 186 students (27% of student body)
Contact: F. Parvin Sharpless, Headmaster

Roland Park Country School
5204 Roland Avenue
Baltimore, MD 21210
(301) 323–5500

Type of School: Girls' day school; 608 students, grades K–12
Tuition: $5,150 to $7,450
$ Given: $417,300
Contact: Margaret E. Smith, Headmistress

St. Paul's School
Brooklandville, MD 21022
(301) 825–4400

Type of School: Episcopal co–ed day school, pre–first through grade 4; Episcopal boys' day school, pre–first through grade 12; 755 students
Tuition: $7,050 to $7,250
$ Given: $431,000 to 174 students (23% of student body)
Contact: Robert Ward Hallett, Headmaster

St. Paul's School for Girls
Falls Road & Seminary Ave.
Brooklandville, MD 21022
(301) 823–6323

Type of School: Episcopal girls' day school; 300 students, grades 5–12
Tuition: $7,000
$ Given: $230,000 to 78 students (26% of student body)
Contact: Lila B. Lohr, Headmistress

Severn School
Water Street
Severna Park, MD 21146
(301) 647–7700

Type of School: Co–ed day school; 473 students, grades 6–12
Tuition: $6,600
$ Given: $206,000 to 64 students (14% of student body)
Contact: Robert W. Gray, Director of Administration

MASSACHUSETTS

Bancroft School
110 Shore Drive
Worcester, MA 01605
(508) 853–2640

Type of School: Co–ed day school; 510 students, grades K–12
Tuition: $4,150 to $8,200
$ Given: $245,000 to 117 students (23% of student body)
Contact: Marigolden G. Tritschler, Head of School

Belmont Hill School
350 Prospect Street
Belmont, MA 02178
(617) 484–4410

Type of School: Day and 5–day boarding school for boys; 405 students, grades 7–12
Tuition: $14,350 (5–day boarding); $11,500 (day)
$ Given: $390,000 to 89 students (22% of student body)

Berkshire School
Undermountain Road
Sheffield, MA 01257
(413) 229–8511

Type of School: Co–ed boarding and day school; 411 students, grades 9–12
Tuition: $15,100 (boarding); $9,500 (day)
$ Given: $1,010,000 to 144 students (35% of student body)
Contact: David B. Reece, Director of Administration

• • • • • • • • • • • • • • • • • • •

Boston College High School
150 Morrissey Boulevard
Dorchester, MA 02125
(617) 436-3900

Type of School: Boys' day school; 1,200 students, grades 9–12
Tuition: $4,100
$ Given: $400,000 to 276 students (23% of student body)
Contact: The Rev. Joseph R. Fahey, S.J., President

Brooks School
1160 Great Pond Road
North Andover, MA 01845
(508) 686-6101

Type of School: Co-ed boarding and day school; 312 students, grades 9–12
Tuition: $15,950 (boarding); $11,400 (day)
$ Given: $740,000
Contact: Lawrence W. Becker, Headmaster

Commonwealth School
151 Commonwealth Avenue
Boston, MA 02116
(617) 266-7525

Type of School: Co-ed day school; 112 students, grades 9–12
Tuition: $11,500
$ Given: $290,000 to 37 students (33% of student body)
Contact: Rebecca Folkman and Robert Vollrath, Directors of Administration

Dana Hall
45 Dana Road
Wellesley, MA 02181
(617) 235-3010

Type of School: Girls' boarding (grades 9–12) and day (grades 6–12) school; 330 students
Tuition: $16,725 (boarding); $12,075 (day)
$ Given: $650,000 to 96 students (29% of student body)
Contact: Mrs. Elaine Wiswall Betts, Headmistress

Deerfield Academy
Deerfield, MA 01342
(413) 772-0241

Type of School: Co-ed boarding and day school; 577 students, grades 9–12
Tuition: $14,900 (boarding); $10,500 (day)
$ Given: $1,400,000 to 196 students (34% of student body)
Contact: Michael S. Cary, Dean of Administration

Eaglebrook School
Pine Nook Road
Deerfield, MA 01342
(413) 774–7411

Type of School: Day school for boys and several faculty daughters; boarding school for boys; 248 students, grades 6–9
Tuition: $17,900 (boarding); $10,850 (day)
$ Given: $440,000 to 60 students (24% of student body)
Contact: Theodore J. Low, Director of Administration

Governor Dummer Academy
Byfield, MA 01922
(508) 465–1763

Type of School: Co–ed boarding and day school; 347 students, grades 6–9
Tuition: $15,350 (boarding); $10,400 (day)
$ Given: $750,000 to 83 students (24% of student body)
Contact: Michael A. Moonves, Director of Administration

Groton School
P.O. Box 991
Groton, MA 01450
(508) 448–3363

Type of School: Co–ed boarding and day school; 320 students, grades 8–12
Tuition: $15,200 (boarding); $10,500 (day)
$ Given: $850,000 to 115 students (36% of student body)
Contact: William M. Polk, Headmaster

Noble & Greenough School
507 Bridge Street
Dedham, MA 02026
(617) 326–3700

Type of School: Co–ed five–day boarding school; 460 students, grades 7–12
Tuition: $13,000 (boarding); $10,000 (day)
$ Given: $835,000 to 143 students (31% of student body)
Contact: Richard H. Baker, Headmaster

Northfield Mount Hermon School
Northfield, MA 01360
(413) 498–5311

Type of School: Co–ed; 1020 students, grades 9–12
Tuition: $14,800 (boarding); $9,600 (day)
$ Given: $2,816,000 to 388 students (38% of student body)
Contact: Virginia M. de Veer, Director of Administration

Phillips Academy
Main Street
Andover, MA 01810
(508) 475–3400

Type of School: Co–ed; 1,200 students, grades 9–12
Tuition: $13,500 (boarding); $10,300 (day)
$ Given: $4,600,000 to 564 students (47% of student body)

The Roxbury Latin School
St. Theresa Avenue
West Roxbury, MA 02132

Type of School: Boys' day school; 274 students, grades 7–12
Tuition: $7,400
$ Given: $465,625 to 104 students (38% of student body)
Contact: The Rev. F. Washington Jarvis, Headmaster

Tabor Academy
Front Street
Marion, MA 02738
(508) 748–2000

Type of School: Co–ed boarding and day school; 465 students, grades 9–12
Tuition: $16,000 (boarding); $11,100 (day)
$ Given: $850,000 to 116 students (25% of student body)
Contact: Carl J. Lovejoy, Director of Administration

Thayer Academy
745 Washington Street
Braintree, MA 02184
(617) 843–3580

Type of School: Co–ed day school; 570 students, grades 6–12
Tuition: $9,800
$ Given: $850,000
Contact: Peter J. Benelli, Headmaster

Wilbraham & Monson Academy
Wilbraham, MA 01095
(413) 596–6811

Type of School: Co–ed boarding (grades 8–13) and day (grades 7–13) school; 203 students
Tuition: $15,000 (boarding); $8,700 (day)
$ Given: $362,663 to 61 students (30% of student body)
Contact: Stoddard M. Wilson, Director of Administration

The Windsor School
Pilgrim Road
Boston, MA 02215
(617) 735–9500

Type of School: Girls' day school; 370 students, grades 5–12
Tuition: $10,350 to $11,100
$ Given: $450,000
Contact: Carolyn McClintock, Director

MICHIGAN

Greenhills School
850 Greenhills Drive
Ann Arbor, MI 48105
(313) 769–4010

Type of School: Co–ed day school; 406 students, grades 6–12
Tuition: $5,525
$ Given: $177,000 to 93 students (23% of student body)
Contact: David T. McDowell, Headmaster

The Grosse Pointe Academy
171 Lake Shore Road
Grosse Pointe Farms, MI 48236
(313) 886–1221

Type of School: Co–ed day school; 425 students, 2-1/2 to 5 years old through grade 8
Tuition: $3,550 to $6,400
$ Given: $145,000 to 30 students (7% of student body)
Contact: Molly McDermott, Director of Administration

Kingsbury School
5000 Hosner Road
Oxford, MI 48051
(313) 628–2571

Type of School: Co–ed day school; 152 students, pre–kindergarten through grade 8
Tuition: $4,225 to $5,100
$ Given: $72,000 to 38 students (25% of student body)
Contact: Richard C. Halsey, Headmaster

The Leelanau School
One Old Homestead Road
Glen Arbor, MI 49636
(616) 334–3072

Type of School: Co–ed boarding and day school; 80 students, grades 8–12
Tuition: $13,200 (boarding); $7,500 (day)
$ Given: $175,000 to 29 students (36% of student body)
Contact: H. Michael Buhler, Director of Administration

Roeper City & Country School
2190 N. Woodward Avenue
Bloomfield Hills, MI 48013
(313) 642–1500

Type of School: Co–ed college preparatory school for gifted children; 500 students, nursery through grade 12
Tuition: $5,685 to $7,885
$ Given: $330,000 to 125 students (25% of student body)
Contact: Dr. Libby Balter Blume, Interim Headmistress

The Valley School
3301 N. Vernon Avenue
Flint, MI 48506–2877
(313) 767–4004

Type of School: Co–ed day school; 165 students, pre–kindergarten through grade 12
Tuition: $3,200 to $6,000
$ Given: $75,000 to 41 students (25% of student body)
Contact: Marianne Russell Kugler, Headmistress

MINNESOTA

The Blake School Upper School
511 Kenwood Parkway
Minneapolis, MN 55403
(612) 339–1700

The Blake School Middle School
110 Blake Road, South
Hopkins, MN 55343
(612) 938–1700

The Blake School Lower School
110 Blake Road, South
Hopkins, MN 55343
(612) 935–6994

The Blake School Highcroft Campus
301 Peavey Lane
Wayzata, MN 55391
(612) 473–1700

Type of School: Co–ed; 1,071 students, kindergarten through grade 12
Tuition: $4,065 to $7,400
$ Given: $995,000 to 193 students (18% of student body)
Contact: Michael Miller, Director of Administration

Breck School
123 Ottawa Avenue, North
Minneapolis, MN 55422
(612) 377–5000

Type of School: Co-ed day school; 1,100 students, pre–school through grade 12
Tuition: $2,800 to $6,820
$ Given: $690,000 to 165 students (15% of student body)
Contact: Michael Weiszel, Director of Administration

Groves Learning Center
3200 Highway 100 South
St. Louis Park, MN 55416

Type of School: Co–ed day school for learning disabled; 156 students, pre–school through grade 12
Tuition: $9,960
$ Given: $100,000 to 33 students (21% of student body)
Contact: Sue Kirchhoff, Head of School

St. John's Preparatory School
Collegeville, MN 56321
(612) 363–3317

Type of School: Roman Catholic boarding and day school for boys; 207 students, grades 9–12
Tuition: $9,995 (boarding); $4,560 (day)
$ Given: $230,000 to 62 students (30% of student body)
Contact: Father Thomas Andert, O.S.B., Headmaster

St. Paul Academy & Summit School
1712 Randolph Avenue
St. Paul, MN 55105
(612) 698–2451

Type of School: Co–ed day school; 820 students, kindergarten through grade 12
Tuition: $7,000
$ Given: $843,000 to 246 students (30% of student body)
Contact: James E. Buckheit, Headmaster

St. Thomas Academy
949 Mendote Heights Road
St. Paul, MN 55120
(612) 454–4570

Type of School: Boys' Roman Catholic college preparatory military day school; 500 students
Tuition: $4,100 to $4,600
$ Given: $250,000 to 130 students (26% of student body)
Contact: John B. Greving, Headmaster

Shattuck – St. Mary's School
P.O. Box 218
1000 Shumway Avenue
Faribault, MN 55021
(507) 334–6466 or
(507) 332–7527

Type of School: Co–ed boarding and day school; 144 students, grades 7–12
Tuition: $13,500 (boarding); $6,750 (day)
$ Given: $35,000 to 56 students (39% of student body)
Contact: Holly G. Hollibaugh, Director of Administration

MISSISSIPPI

All Saints' Episcopal School
Vicksburg, MS 39180
(601) 636–5266

Type of School: Co–ed boarding and day school; 179 students, grades 8–12
Tuition: $10,500 (boarding); $3,200 (day)
$ Given: $90,000 to 32 students (18% of student body)

St. Andrew's Episcopal School
4120 Old Canton Road
Jackson, MS 39216
(601) 982–5065

Type of School: Co–ed day school; 866 students, pre–kindergarten through grade 12
Tuition: $1,800 to $3,950
$ Given: $300,000
Contact: J. Steven Bean, Headmaster

MISSOURI

The Barstow School
11511 Stat Line Road
Kansas City, MO 64114
(816) 942–3255

Type of School: Co–ed college preparatory day school; 455 students, pre–school through grade 12
Tuition: $2,950 to $6,975
$ Given: $250,000 to 118 students (26% of student body)
Contact: James E. Achterberg, Headmaster

John Burroughs School
755 S. Price Road
St. Louis, MO 63124
(314) 993–4040

Type of School: Co–ed college preparatory day school; 562 students, grades 7–12
Tuition: $7,350
$ Given: $500,000 to 152 students (27% of student body)
Contact: Keith E. Shahan, Headmaster

The Pembroke Hill School
400 West 51st Street
Kansas City, MO 64112
(816) 753–1300

Type of School: Co–ed day school; 1,015 students, playground through grade 12
Tuition: $2,880 to $6,585
$ Given: $753,713 to 315 students (31% of student body)
Contact: Thomas D. Harvey, Headmaster

Mary Institute & The Ronald S. Beasly School
101 N. Warson Road
St. Louis, MO 63124
(314) 993–0472

Type of School (Mary Institute): Girls' school, grades 5–12
Type of School (The Ronald S. Beasly School): Co–ed, junior kindergarten through grade 4
Tuition: $4,500 to $7,475
$ Given: $368,000
Contact: Anthony Bramley Fruhauf, Headmaster

Rockhurst High School
Greenlease Memorial Campus
9301 State Line Road
Kansas City, MO 64114
(816) 363–2036

Type of School: Roman Catholic boys' day school; 810 students, grades 9–12
Tuition: $3,000
$ Given: $126,000 to 162 students (20% of student body)
Contact: The Rev. Thomas W. Cummings, S.J.

Saint Louis Country Day School
425 N. Warson Road
St. Louis, MO 63124
(314) 993–5100

Type of School: Boys' college preparatory school; 520 students, grades 5–12
Tuition: $7,500
$ Given: $462,000 to 140 students (27% of student body)
Contact: Duncan L. Marshall, Jr., Director of Administration

St. Louis University High School
4970 Oakland Avenue
St. Louis, MO 63110
(314) 531–0330

Type of School: Roman Catholic boys' day school; 960 students, grades 9–12
Tuition: $2,670
$ Given: $220,000 to 230 students (24% of student body)
Contact: The Rev. James H. Baker, S.J., President

MONTANA

Spring Creek Community
Box 429
Thompson Falls, MT 59873
(406) 827–4344

Type of School: Co–ed boarding school for exceptional children; 45 students, grades 9–12
Tuition: $36,000 for 1st year; $24,000 for 2nd year
$ Given: $80,000 to 5 students (10% of student body)
Additional Information: Family's health insurance may cover all or part of tuition.

NEBRASKA

Brownell–Talbot
400 N. Happy Hollow Boulevard
Omaha, NE 68132
(402) 556–3772

Type of School: Co–ed college preparatory day school; 275 students, pre–kindergarten through grade 12
Tuition: $1,700 to $3,990
$ Given: $120,000 to 82 students (30% of student body)
Contact: Dianne Desler, Headmistress

NEVADA

The Meadows School
8601 Scholar Lane
Las Vegas, NV 89128
(702) 254–1610

Type of School: Co–ed college preparatory day school; 403 students, kindergarten through grade 12
Tuition: $4,500 to $6,000
$ Given: $175,000 to 93 students (23% of student body)
Contact: Dr. LeOre Cobbley, Director of Middle and Upper Schools

NEW HAMPSHIRE

Brewster Academy
Wolfboro, NH 03894
(603) 569–1600

Type of School: Co–ed boarding and day school; 309 students, grades 9–12
Tuition: $16,250 (boarding); $8,650 (day)
$ Given: $533,500 to 62 students (20% of student body)
Contact: Stewart M. Dunlop, Director of Administration

The Derryfield School
2108 N. River Road
Manchester, NH 03104
(603) 669–4524

Type of School: Co–ed day school; 300 students, grades 7–12
Tuition: $7,200
$ Given: $200,350 to 72 students (24% of student body)
Contact: Marcus D. Hurlbutt, Headmaster

Holderness School
Plymouth, NH 03264
(603) 536–1257

Type of School: Co–ed day and boarding school; 260 students, grades 9–12
Tuition: $13,200 (boarding); $6,900 (day)
$ Given: $320,000 to 70 students (27% of student body)
Contact: The Rev. Brinton Woodward, Jr., Headmaster

Kimball Union Academy
Meriden, NH 03770
(603) 469–3211

Type of School: Co–ed boarding school with limited day enrollment; 288 students, grades 9–12
Tuition: $14,200 (boarding); $8,000 (day)
$ Given: $850,000 to 115 students (40% of student body)
Contact: Edward H. Stansfield, Director of Administration

New Hampton Schools
New Hampton, NH 03256
(603) 744–5401

Type of School: Co–ed boarding and day school; 250 students, grades 9–12
Tuition: $16,800 (boarding); $8,500 (day)
$ Given: $440,000 to 73 students (29% of student body)
Contact: Bruce E. Paro, Director of Administration

Phillips Exeter Academy
Exeter, NH 03833
(603) 772–4311

Type of School: Co–ed boarding and day school, grades 9–12
Tuition: $13,500 (boarding); $9,200 (day)
$ Given: $2,750,000
Contact: Kendra Stearns O'Donnell, Principal

St. Paul's School
325 Pleasant Street
Concord, NH 03301
(603) 225–3341

Type of School: Co–ed boarding school; 500 students, grades 9–12
Tuition: $13,500
$ Given: $1,500,000 to 185 students (37% of student body)
Contact: The Rev. Charles H. Clark, Rector

Tilton Schools
Tilton, NH 03276
(603) 286–4342

Type of School: Co–ed boarding and day school; 232 students, grades 9–12
Tuition: $16,000 (boarding); $9,200 (day)
$ Given: $420,000 to 67 students (29% of student body)
Contact: Michael E. Baker, Headmaster

NEW JERSEY

Blair Academy
Blairstown, NJ 07825
(908) 362-6121

Type of School: Co-ed boarding and day school; 359 students, grades 9–12
Tuition: $14,700 (boarding); $9,500 (day)
$ Given: $615,900 to 85 students (24% of student body)

The High School of Princeton
Edgerstowne Road
P.O. Box 271
Princeton, NJ 08542
(609) 921-7600

Type of School: Co-ed boarding (grades 9–12) and day (grades 6–8) school; 498 students
Tuition: $14,995 (boarding); $9,600 (day)
$ Given: $410,000 to 75 students (15% of student body)
Contact: P. Terence Beach, Director of Administration

The Lawrenceville School
Lawrenceville, NJ 08648
(609) 896-0400 or
(800) 735-2035

Type of School: Co-ed boarding and day school; 761 students, grades 8–12
Tuition: $14,000 (boarding); $10,250 (day)
$ Given: $1,580,650 in scholarships and $150,000 in loans to 190 students (25% of student body)
Contact: Philip G. Pratt, Director of Administration

The Montclair Kimberley Academy
201 Valley Road
Montclair, NJ 07042
(201) 746-9800

Type of School: Co-ed day school; 1,050 students, kindergarten through grade 12
Tuition: $7,000 to $9,500
$ Given: $900,000 to 262 students (25% of student body)
Contact: Frances R. O'Connor, Principal

Morristown-Beard School
Whippanx Road
P.O. Box 1999
Morristown, NJ 07962-1999
(201) 539-3032

Type of School: Co-ed day school; 415 students, grades 7–12
Tuition: $9,475 (middle); $9,700 (upper)
$ Given: $300,000 to 95 students (23% of student body)
Contact: James J. Chudomel, Director of Administration

Newark Academy
91 S. Orange Avenue
Livingston, NJ 07039
(201) 992–7000

Type of School: Co–ed day school; 485 students, grades 6–12
Tuition: $9,500
$ Given: $300,000 to 107 students (22% of student body)
Contact: Elaine R. Cooper, Director of Administration

Peddie School
South Main Street
Highstown, NJ 08520
(609) 448–0997

Type of School: Co–ed boarding and day school; 520 students, grades 8–12
Tuition: $14,000 (boarding); $9,000 (day)
$ Given: $800,000 to 104 students (20% of student body)
Contact: John Martin, Director of Administration

The Pennington School
112 W. Delaware Avenue
Pennington, NJ 08534
(609) 737–1838

Type of School: Co–ed boarding and day school; 325 students, grades 7–12
Tuition: $15,100 (boarding); $9,600 (day)
$ Given: $385,000 to 72 students (22% of student body)
Contact: Diane P. Monteleone, Director of Administration

Princeton Day School
P.O. Box 75
The Great Road
Princeton, NJ 08542
(609) 924–6700

Type of School: Co–ed day school; 500 students, junior kindergarten through 12
Tuition: $7,850 to $9,100
$ Given: $875,000 to 224 students (28% of student body)
Contact: Duncan Wells Allins, Headmaster

Rutgers Preparatory School
1345 Easton Avenue
Somerset, NJ 08873
(201) 545–5600

Type of School: Co–ed day school, pre–kindergarten through grade 12
Tuition: $6,200 to $8,950
$ Given: $385,000
Contact: Edward C. Lingenheld, Headmaster

NEW MEXICO

Albuquerque Academy
6400 Wyoming Blvd., NE
Albuquerque, NM 87109
(505) 828–3200

Type of School: Co–ed day school; 848 students, grades 6–12
Tuition: $5,150
$ Given: $925,000 to 305 students (36% of student body)
Contact: Robert L. Bovinette, Headmaster

New Mexico Military Institute
North Hill
Roswell, NM 88201
(800) 445–0908
(in New Mexico)
(800) 421–5376
(outside New Mexico)

Type of School: Co–ed boarding school; 966 students, grades 9–12
Tuition: $650 to $1,600
$ Given: $500,000 to 589 students (61% of student body)
Contact: Col. Donald S. Stuart, Superintendent

Rio Grande School
715 Camino Cabra
Santa Fe, NM 87501
(505) 983–1621

Type of School: Co–ed day school; 103 students, kindergarten through grade 6
Tuition: $5,500
$ Given: $15,000 to 19 students (18% of student body)
Contact: Margaret A. Anderson, Head of School

Sandia Preparatory School
532 Osuna Road, NE
Albuquerque, NM 87113
(505) 344–1671

Type of School: Co–ed day school; 350 students, grades 6–12
Tuition: $5,200
$ Given: $235,000 to 98 students (28% of student body)
Contact: Richard L. Heath, Headmaster

Santa Fe Preparatory School
1101 Camino de la Cruz Blanca
Santa Fe, NM 87501
(505) 982–1829

Type of School: Co–ed day school; 200 students, grades 7–12
Tuition: $5,725
$ Given: $113,000 to 50 students (25% of student body)
Contact: Stephen M. Machen, Ph.D., Headmaster

NEW YORK

The Brearley School
610 East 83rd Street
New York, NY 10028
(212) 744–8582

Type of School: Girls' day school; 626 students, kindergarten through grade 12
Tuition: $7,800 to $10,200
$ Given: Loan program, plus $830,000 to 188 students (30% of student body)
Contact: Evelyn J. Halpert, Head of School

The Chapin School
100 E. End Avenue
New York, NY 10028
(212) 744–2335

Type of School: Girls' day school; 581 students, grades K–12
Tuition: $8,500 to $10,800
$ Given: $705,350 to 163 students (28% of student body)
Contact: Mildred Berendsen, Headmistress

The Dalton School
108 East 89th Street
New York, NY 10128
(212) 722–5160

Type of School: Co–ed day school; 1,250 students, kindergarten through grade 12
Tuition: $9,600 to $10,860
$ Given: $1,700,000 to 350 students (28% of student body)
Contact: Gardner P. Dunman, Headmaster

Emma Willard School
Troy, NY 12180
(518) 274–4440

Type of School: Girls' boarding and day school; 239 students, grades 9–12
Tuition: $15,000 (boarding); $8,700 (day)
$ Given: $740,000 to 96 students (40% of student body)
Contact: Mary Jo Driscoll, Director of Administration

The Ethical Culture/ Fieldston Schools
33 Central Park West
New York, NY 10023
(212) 874–5205

Fieldston Rd. & Manhattan College Parkways
Riverdale, NY 10471
(212) 543–5000

Type of School: Co–ed; 1,500 students, pre–kindergarten through grade 6 (Manhattan, Lower School and The Fieldston School) and grades 7–12 (The Bronx)
Tuition: $7,400 to $10,350
$ Given: $2,000,000 to 450 students (30% of student body)
Contact: Howard B. Radest, Director

Horace Mann – Barnard School
231 West 246th Street
Bronx, NY 10471
(212) 548–4000

Type of School: Co–ed day school; 926 students, grades 7–12
Tuition: $10,420
$ Given: $900,000 to 222 students (24% of student body)
Contact: R. Insler Clark, Jr., President

The Masters School
49 Clinton Avenue
Dobbs Ferry, NY 10522
(914) 693–1400

Type of School: Girls' boarding (grades 9–12) and day (grades 6–12) school; 236 students
Tuition:$16,550 (boarding); $9,925 (middle day); $10,550 (upper day)
$ Given: $476,000 to 66 students (28% of student body)
Contact: Sandra M. Moore, Director of Administration

Oakwood School
Poughkeepsie, NY 12601
(914) 462–4200

Type of School: Co–ed boarding and day school; 102 students, grades 9–12
Tuition: $14,800 (7–day boarding); $13,700 (5–day boarding); $9,300 (day)
$ Given: $400,000 to 41 students (40% of student body)
Contact: Brian Fry, Director of Administration

The Packer Collegiate Institute
170 Joralemon Street
Brooklyn, NY 11201
(718) 875–6644

Type of School: Co–ed day school; 690 students, pre–school through grade 12
Tuition: $4,500 to $9,700
$ Given: $1,000,000 to 242 students (35% of student body)
Contact: Dorothy Hutcheson, Interim Headmaster

Polytechnic Preparatory Country Day School
92nd Street & Seventh Ave.
Brooklyn, NY 11228
(718) 836–9800

Type of School: Co–ed day school; 650 students, grades 5–12
Tuition: $9,700 to $10,500
$ Given: $830,000 to 182 students (28% of student body)
Contact: William Magavern Williams, Headmaster

Riverdale Country School
5250 Fieldston Road
Bronx, NY 10471–2999
(212) 549–8810

Type of School: Co–ed day school; 830 students, pre-kindergarten through grade 12
Tuition: $9,500 to $11,500
$ Given: $1,036,460 to 224 students (27% of student body)
Contact: Roger B. Boocock, Headmaster

The Stony Brook School
Stony Brook, NY 11790
(516) 751–1800

Type of School: Co–ed boarding and day school; 344 students, grades 7–12
Tuition: $14,000 (boarding); $9,500 (day)
$ Given: $650,000 to 107 students (31% of student body)
Contact: Karl Soderstrom, Headmaster

Trinity School
139 West 91st Street
New York, NY 10024
(212) 873–1650

Type of School: Co–ed day school; 899 students, grades K–12
Tuition: $10,465 to $12,355
$ Given: $899,105 to 216 students (24% of student body)
Contact: Christopher Berrisford, Headmaster

NORTH CAROLINA

The Asheville School
Asheville, NC 28806
(704) 254–6345

Type of School: Co–ed boarding and day school; 205 students, grades 9–12
Tuition: $12,500 (boarding); $7,400 (day)
$ Given: $221,000 to 29 students (14% of student body)
Contact: Jeremiah W. Jones, Director of Administration

Carolina Friends School
Route 1, Box 183
Durham, NC 27705
(919) 929–1800
or 383–6602

Type of School: Co–ed day school; 400 students, pre-school through grade 12
Tuition: $2,148 to $4,595
$ Given: $160,735 to 108 students (27% of student body)
Contact: John Baird, Principal

Charlotte Country Day School
1440 Carmel Road
Charlotte, NC 28226
(704) 366–1241

Type of School: Co–ed day school; 1,427 students, junior kindergarten through grade 12
Tuition: $3,050 to $6,500
$ Given: $254,900 to 271 students (19% of student body)
Contact: Fanny Cracknell, Director of Administration

Charlotte Latin School
P.O. Box 6143
Charlotte, NC 28207
(704) 846–1100

Type of School: Co–ed day school; 1,000 students, pre–kindergarten through grade 12
Tuition: $3,190 to $5,695
$ Given: $296,905 to 220 students (22% of student body)
Contact: E.J. Fox, Jr., Headmaster

Greensboro Day School
5401 Lawndale Drive
Greensboro, NC 27429–0361
(919) 288–8590

Type of School: Co–ed; 750 students, kindergarten through grade 12
Tuition: $3,000 to $5,550
$ Given: $368,876 to 202 students (27% of student body)
Contact: D. Ralph Davison, Jr., Headmaster

Salem Academy
500 Salem Avenue
Winston–Salem, NC 27108
(919) 721–2644

Type of School: Girls' boarding and day school; 158 students, grades 9–12
Tuition: $14,550 (boarding); $7,000 (day)
$ Given: $185,000 to 40 students (25% of student body)
Contact: Beth Trice, Director of Administration

The Summit School
2100 Reynolds Road
Winston–Salem, NC 27106
(919) 722–2777

Type of School: Co–ed day school; 660 students, pre–kindergarten through grade 9
Tuition: $3,500 to $5,200
$ Given: $174,000 to 139 students (21% of student body)
Contact: Sandra P. Adams, Headmistress

Westchester Academy
204 Pine Tree Lane
High Point, NC 27265
(919) 869–2128

Type of School: Co–ed day school; 225 students, grades K–12
Tuition: $2,000 to $4,150
$ Given: $115,000 to 72 students (30% of student body)
Contact: George S. Swope, Jr., Interim Headmaster

OHIO

Cincinnati Country Day School
6905 Given Road
Cincinnati, OH 45243–2898
(513) 561–7298

Type of School: Co–ed; 700 students, pre–primary and Montessori (age 3) through grade 12
Tuition: $3,124 to $6,620
$ Given: $437,500 to 196 students (28% of student body)
Contact: John Raushenbush, Headmaster

Hawken School
Lower & Middle Schools
Clubside Road
Lyndhurst, OH 44124
(216) 382–8800

Type of School: Day school; 810 students, kindergarten through grade 12
Tuition: $5,600 to $7,875
$ Given: $670,000 to 219 students (27% of student body)
Contact: T. Douglas Stenberg, Headmaster

Hawken School
Upper School
County Line Road
Gates Mills, OH 44040
(216) 423–4446

Type of School: Day school; 810 students, kindergarten through grade 12
Tuition: $5,600 to $7,875
$ Given: $670,000 to 219 students (27% of student body)
Contact: T. Douglas Stenberg, Headmaster

Maumee Valley Country Day School
1715 S. Reynolds Road
Toledo, OH 43614
(419) 381–1313

Type of School: Co–ed day school; 500 students, pre–kindergarten through grade 12
Tuition: $5,290 to $7,240
$ Given: $470,000 to 150 students (30% of student body)
Contact: C. Richard Cardigan, Interim Head

St. Ignatius High School
1911 West 30th Street
Cleveland, OH 44113
(216) 651–0222

Type of School: Roman Catholic boys' day school; 1,250 students, grades 9–12
Tuition: $3,600
$ Given: $470,000 to 313 students (25% of student body)
Contact: The Rev. Robert J. Welsh, S.J., President

The Seven Hills Schools
5400 Red Bank Road
Cincinnati, OH 45227
(513) 271–9027

Type of School: Co–ed; 915 students, pre–school through grade 12
Tuition: $3,200 to $6,500
$ Given: $506,000 to 238 students (26% of student body)
Contact: Henry P. Briggs, Jr.

University School
Lower School
20701 Brantley Road
Shaker Heights, OH 44122
(216) 321–8260

Type of School: Boys' school; 800 students, kindergarten through grade 12
Tuition: $5,300 to $8,000
$ Given: $640,000 to 216 students (27% of student body)
Contact: Richard A. Hawley, Headmaster

University School
Upper School
Som Center Road
Hunting Valley
Chagrin Falls, OH 44022
(216) 831–2200

Type of School: Boys' school; 800 students, kindergarten through grade 12
Tuition: $5,300 to $8,000
$ Given: $640,000 to 216 students (27% of student body)
Contact: Richard A. Hawley, Headmaster

Western Reserve Academy
Hudson, OH 44236
(216) 650–4400

Type of School: Co–ed boarding and day school; 365 students, grades 9–12
Tuition: $12,700 (boarding); $8,700 (day)
$ Given: $800,000 to 106 students (29% of student body)
Contact: Timothy L. Trautman, Director of Administration

OKLAHOMA

Casady School
P.O. Box 20390
9500 N. Pennsylvania Ave.
Oklahoma City, OK 73156
(405) 755–0550

Type of School: Episcopal co–ed day school; 1,000 students, pre–school through grade 12
Tuition: $2,915 to $5,935
$ Given: $600,000 to 175 students (18% of student body)
Contact: Thomas T. Tongue, Director of Administration

Heritage Hall School
1401 N.W. 115th Street
Oklahoma City, OK 73114
(405) 751–6797

Type of School: Co–ed day school; 818 students, pre–school through grade 12
Tuition: $2,710 to $5,050
$ Given: $235,000 to 213 students (26% of student body)
Contact: Guy A. Bramble, Headmaster

Holland Hall School
5666 E. 81st Street
Tulsa, OK 74137–2099
(918) 481–1111

Type of School: Co–ed college preparatory Episcopal-affiliated day school; 998 students, pre–school through grade 12
Tuition: $1,075 to $5,885
$ Given: Funding to 199 students (20% of student body)
Contact: Nancy Caruthers, Director of Administration

Westminister Day School
4400 N. Shartel
Oklahoma City, OK 73118
(405) 524–0631

Type of School: Co–ed day school; 550 students, pre–school through grade 8
Tuition: $1,900 to $4,150
$ Given: $86,000 to 110 students (20% of student body)
Contact: Charlotte W. Gibbens, Head of School

OREGON

The Catlin Gabel School
8825 S.W. Barnes Road
Portland, OR 97225
(503) 297–1894

Type of School: Co–ed college preparatory day school; 625 students, pre–school through grade 12
Tuition: $3,300 to $7,500
$ Given: $300,000 to 150 students (24% of student body)
Contact: James K. Scott, Headmaster

The Delphian School
20950 S.W. Rock Creek Rd.
Sheridan, OR 97378
(503) 843–3521

Type of School: Co–ed boarding and day school; 146 students, lower school through grade 12
Tuition: $15,200 (boarding); $7,580 (day)
$ Given: Available
Contact: Sharon Fry, Director of Administration, (800) 626–6610

Oregon Episcopal School
6300 S.W. Nicol Road
Portland, OR 97223
(503) 246–7771

Type of School: Co–ed boarding and day school; 628 students, pre–school through grade 12 (day), and grades 9–12 (boarding)
Tuition: $2,915 to $7,780 (day); $14,575 (boarding)
$ Given: $517,030 to 157 students (19.5% of student body)
Contact: Sue Nicol, Director of Administration

Sunriver Preparatory School
P.O. Box 4425
Sunriver, OR 97707
(503) 593–1244

Type of School: Co–ed day school; 150 students, grades K–12
Tuition: $3,970 to $4,980
$ Given: $30,000 to 29 students (19% of student body)
Contact: Gregory Zeigler, Headmaster

PENNSYLVANIA

The Agnes Irwin School
Ithan Avenue
Rosemount, PA
(215) 525–8400

Type of School: College preparatory day school for girls; 520 students, kindergarten through grade 12
Tuition: $5,200 to $8,100
$ Given: $350,000 to 130 students (25% of student body)
Contact: Priscilla S. Watson

Friends' Central School
68th Street & City Avenue
Philadelphia, PA 19151
(215) 649–7440
or
228 Gulph Road
Wynnewood, PA 19096
(215) 642–7575

Type of School: Co–ed day school; 668 students, pre–kindergarten through grade 12
Tuition: $6,145 to $8,840
$ Given: $802,000 to 207 students (31% of student body)
Contact: David M. Felsen, Headmaster

George School
Newton, PA 18940
(215) 968–3811

Type of School: Co–ed Quaker boarding and day school; 514 students, grades 9–12
Tuition: $13,500 (boarding); $8,600 (day)
$ Given: $1,200,000 to 170 students (33% of student body)
Contact: Karen Suplee Howwell, Director of Administration

Germantown Friends School
31 W. Coulter Street
Philadelphia, PA 19144
(215) 951–2300

Type of School: Co–ed Quaker college preparatory day school; 883 students, kindergarten through grade 12
Tuition: $4,850 to $7,870
$ Given: $908,279 to 274 students (31% of student body)
Contact: John A. Wilkinson, Head of School

The Hill School
Pottstown, PA 19464
(215) 326–1000

Type of School: Boarding and day school for boys; 470 students, grades 8–12
Tuition: $14,000 (boarding); $9,000 (day)
$ Given: $852,955 to 146 students (31% of student body)
Contact: Edward M. Kowalchick, Director of Administration

The Mercerburg Academy
Mercerburg, PA 17236
(717) 328–2151

Type of School: Co–ed boarding school; 353 students, grades 9–12
Tuition: $13,500 (boarding); $8,500 (day)
$ Given: $775,550 to 98 students (28% of student body)
Contact: Gordon D. Vink, Jr., Director of Administration

St. Joseph's Preparatory School
1733 W. Girard Avenue
Philadelphia, PA 19130
(215) 978–1950

Type of School: Boys' Roman Catholic day school; 750 students, grades 9–12
Tuition: $6,850 plus books
$ Given: $900,000 to 248 students (33% of student body)
Contact: Albert Zimmerman, Director of Administration

Westtown School
Westtown, PA 19395
(215) 399-0123

Type of School: Quaker co-ed boarding and day school; 463 students, grades 9–12 (boarding) and 6–10 (day)
Tuition: $13,600 (boarding); $6,300 to $7,700 (day)
$ Given: $1,000,000 to 162 students (35% of student body)
Contact: Henry C. Horne, Director of Administration

William Penn Charter School
3000 W. School House Ln.
Philadelphia, PA 19144
(215) 844-3460

Type of School: Quaker-affiliated co-ed day school; 805 students, grades K–12
Tuition: $5,650 to $8,550
$ Given: $1,000,000
Contact: Earl J. Ball III, Headmaster

Wyoming Seminary College Preparatory School
Sprague Avenue
Kingston, PA 18704
(717) 283-6060

Type of School: Co-ed boarding and day school; 311 students, grades 9–12
Tuition: $14,150 (boarding); $6,850 (day)
$ Given: $900,000 to 105 students (34% of student body)
Contact: John R. Eidam, Dean of Administration

RHODE ISLAND

Lincoln School
301 Butler Avenue
Providence, RI 01906
(401) 331-9696

Type of School: Quaker girls' day school; 400 students, nursery through grade 12
Tuition: $7,850
$ Given: $260,000 to 92 students (23% of student body)
Contact: B. Barbara Boerner, Headmistress

Moses Brown School
250 Lloyd Avenue
Providence, RI 02906
(401) 831-7350

Type of School: Friends co-ed college preparatory day school; 755 students, nursery through grade 12
Tuition: $13,400 (boarding); $3,500 to $7,700 (day)
$ Given: $595,600 to 189 students (25% of student body)
Contact: David Campbell Burnham, Headmaster

Portsmouth Abbey School
Cory's Lane
Portsmouth, RI 02871
(401) 683–2000

Type of School: Roman Catholic college preparatory boarding and day school for boys; 238 students
Tuition: $14,230 (boarding); $8,000 (day)
$ Given: $475,000 to 69 students (29% of student body)
Contact: Holly Hartge, Acting Director of Administration

Providence Country Day School
2117 Pawtucket Avenue
East Providence, RI 02914
(401) 438–5170

Type of School: Boys' (grades 5–12) and girls' (grades 9–12) school; 208 students
Tuition: $8,200 to $8,600
$ Given: $302,000 to 67 students (32% of student body)
Contact: Porter D. Caesar II, Headmaster

Rocky Hill School
Ives Road
East Greenwich, RI 02818
(401) 884–9070

Type of School: Co–ed day school; 278 students, nursery through grade 12
Tuition: $2,000 to $7,600
$ Given: $375,000 to 120 students (43% of student body)
Contact: Alan F. Flynn, Jr., Headmaster

St. Andrew's School
63 Federal Road
Barrington, RI 02806
(401) 246–1230

Type of School: Co–ed boarding and day school; 125 students, grades 6–12
Tuition: $8,600 (boarding); $8,450 to $8,900 (day)
$ Given: $280,000 to 31 students (25% of student body)
Contact: Andrea C.C. Martin, Director of Administration

St. George's School
Middletown, RI 02840
(401) 847–7565

Type of School: Episcopal preparatory co–ed; 320 students, grades 9–12
Tuition: $15,200 (boarding); $9,100 (day)
$ Given: $680,000 to 102 students (32% of student body)
Contact: Charles A. Hamblet, Headmaster

The Wheeler School/ Hamilton School
216 Hope Street
Providence, RI 02906
(401) 421–8100

Type of School: Wheeler: co–ed day school; Hamilton: co–ed day school for high–potential language disabled students; 662 students, nursery through grade 12
Tuition: $3,800 to $7,700 (Wheeler); $11,200 (Hamilton)
$ Given: $569,300 to 172 students (26% of student body)
Contact: William C. Prescott, Jr., Headmaster

SOUTH CAROLINA

Aiken Prerparatory School
Box 317
Aiken, SC 29802
(803) 648–3223

Type of School: Co–ed day shool (100 students), 4-year kindergarten through grade 9; boys' boarding school (40 students), grades 4–9
Tuition: $10,900 (boarding); $2,500 to $4,400 (day)
$ Given: $70,000 to 32 students (23% of student body)
Contact: David J. Devey, Headmaster

Hammond School
854 Galway Lane
Columbia, SC 29209
(803) 776–0295

Type of School: Co–ed day school; 538 students, 4-year kindergarten through grade 12
Tuition: $1,500 to $3,850
$ Given: $100,000 to 118 students (22% of student body)
Contact: Mary Ann Eubanks, Director of Administration

Hilton Head Preparatory School
8 Fox Grape Road
Hilton Head Island, SC 29928
(803) 671–2286

Type of School: Co–ed day school; 350 students, grades 1-12
Tuition: $3,600 to $4,700
$ Given: $160,000 to 91 students (26% of student body)
Contact: Bobby W. Welch, Headmaster

Porter Gaud School
Albemarle Point
Charleston, SC 29407
(803) 556–3620

Type of School: Co–ed day school; 775 students, grades 1–12
Tuition: $4,275 to $5,245
$ Given: $22,755 to 124 students (16% of student body)
Contact: Gordon E. Bondurant, Headmaster

The Spartanburg Day School
1701 Skylyn Drive
Spartanburg, SC 29302
(803) 582–7539

Type of School: Co–ed day school; 498 students, kindergarten through grade 12
Tuition: $1,700 to $3,640
$ Given: $75,000 to 104 students (21% of student body)
Contact: Gary E. Clark, Headmaster

TENNESSEE

The Baylor School
Willimas Island Ferry Road
P.O. Box 1337
Chattanooga, TN 37401
(615) 267–8505

Type of School: Co–ed boarding and day school; 524 students, grades 9–12 (boarding) and 7–12 (day)
Tuition: $12,800 (boarding); $6,500 (day)
$ Given: $575,000 to 94 students (18% of student body)
Contact: Scott Wilson, Director of Administration

Girls Preparatory School
200 Barton Avenue
Chattanooga, TN 37405
(615) 267–0033

Type of School: Girls' day school; 582 students, grades 7–12
Tuition: $4,650
$ Given: $244,000 to 140 students (24% of student body)
Contact: Stanley R. Tucker, Jr., Headmaster

Grace – St. Luke's Episcopal School
246 S. Belvedere Boulevard
Memphis, TN 38104
(901) 278–0200

Type of School: Co–ed day school; pre–kindergarten through grade 9
Tuition: $1,590 to $4,155
$ Given: $186,000
Contact: E. John Effinger, Headmaster

The McCallie School
Missionary Ridge
Chattanooga, TN 37404
(615) 622–2163

Type of School: College preparatory boarding and day school for boys; 702 students, grades 9–12 (boarding) and 7–12 (day)
Tuition: $12,800 (boarding); $6,400 (day)
$ Given: $700,000 to 140 students (20% of student body)
Contact: Steven B. Hearn, Director of Administration

Memphis University School
6191 Park Avenue
Memphis, TN 38119

Type of School: Boys' day school; 575 students, grades 7–12
Tuition: $5,085
$ Given: $260,000
Contact: D. Eugene Thorn, Headmaster

St. Andrew's Sewanee School
St. Andrews, TN 37372
(615) 598–5651

Type of School: Episcopal co–ed day and boarding school; 237 students, grades 7–12 (day) and 9–12 (boarding)
Tuition: $11,500 (boarding); $4,450 to $4,650 (day)
$ Given: $250,000 to 90 students (38% of student body)
Contact: Harriet Govan Yaun, Director of Administration

The Webb School
Highway 82
Bell Buckle, TN 37020
(615) 389–6003

Type of School: Co–ed boarding and day school; 147 students, grades 7–12
Tuition: $11,800 (boarding); $4,800 (day)
$ Given: $190,300 to 49 students (33% of student body)
Contact: Larry W. Nichols, Director of Administration

Webb School of Knoxville
9800 Webb School Drive
Knoxville, TN 37923
(615) 693–0011

Type of School: Co–ed day school; 732 students, grades 5–12
Tuition: $5,090
$ Given: $202,700 to 146 students (20% of student body)
Contact: William B. Pfeiffer, President

TEXAS

Cistercian Preparatory School
One Cistercian Road
Irving, TX 75039
(214) 438–4956

Type of School: Roman Catholic day school for boys; 312 students, grades 5–12
Tuition: $4,600 to $4,950
$ Given: $235,000 to 96 students (31% of student body)
Contact: Fr. Bernard Marton, Headmaster

Fort Worth Country Day School
4200 Country Day Lane
Fort Worth, TX 76109
(817) 732–7718

Type of School: Co–ed; 845 students, kindergarten through grade 12
Tuition: $4,700 to $5,800
$ Given: $275,000 to 177 students (21% of student body)
Contact: Geoffrey C. Butler, Headmaster

Greenhill School
14255 Midway Road
Dallas, TX 75244
(214) 661–1211

Type of School: Co–ed day school; 1,160 students, pre-school through grade 12
Tuition: $2,855 to $6,545
$ Given: $650,000 to 140 students (12% of student body)
Contact: Steve Blanchard, Director of Administration

The Hockaday School
P.O. Box 299000
11600 Welch Road
Dallas, TX 75229–2999
(214) 363–6311

Type of School: Girls' boarding and day school; 897 students, grades 8–12 (boarding and day), and pre–school through grade 7 (day only)
Tuition: $17,500 (boarding); $3,415—$9,500 (day)
$ Given: $454,000 to 77 students (9% of student body)
Contact: Judy Gass, Director of Administration

The Kinkaid School
201 Kinkaid School Drive
Houston, TX 77024
(713) 782–1640

Type of School: Co–ed day school; 1,250 students, nursery through grade 12
Tuition: $2,360 to $5,800
$ Given: Over $380,000 to 90 students (7% of student body)
Contact: Robert W. Beck, Jr., Director of Administration

St. John's School
2401 Claremont Lane
Houston, TX 77019
(713) 850–0222

Type of School: Co–ed day school; 1,144 students, grades K–12
Tuition: $5,085 to $6,300
$ Given: $430,000 to 252 students (22% of student body)
Contact: James R. Maggart, Headmaster

St. Stephen's Episcopal School
P.O. Box 1868
Austin, TX 78767
(512) 327–1213

Type of School: Co–ed day and boarding school; 292 students, grades 7–12 (day) and 9–12 (boarding)
Tuition: $12,470 (boarding); $6,570 to $7,270 (day)
$ Given: $367,725 to 58 students (20% of student body)
Contact: Steven Ruzicka, Director of Administration

Trinity Valley School
6101 McCart Avenue
Fort Worth, TX 76133
(817) 292–6060

Type of School: Co–ed day school; 689 students, grades K–12
Tuition: $4,350 to $5,450
$ Given: $231,000
Contact: Judith S. Kinser, Director of Administration

UTAH

Rowland Hall – St. Mark's School Lower School
205 1st Avenue
Salt Lake City, UT 84103
(801) 355–7485

Upper School
843 Lincoln Street
Salt Lake City, UT 84102
(801) 355–7494

Type of School: Co–ed day school; 825 students, pre–kindergarten through grade 12
Tuition: $4,150 to $4,850
$ Given: $160,000 to 157 students (19% of student body)
Contact (Lower School): Karen Hyde, Director of Administration
Contact (Upper School): Mary Beth Beck, Director of Administration

Wasatch Academy
P.O. Box Department B
120 South
100 West
Mount Pleasant, UT 84647
(801) 462–2411

Type of School: Presbyterian-related co–ed boarding and day school; 120 students, grades 9–12
Tuition: $14,500 (boarding); $4,000 (day)
$ Given: Funding to 20 students (17% of total) as determined by the Student Scholarship Service
Contact: Jodi Tuttle, Director of Administration

VERMONT

The Putney School
Putney, VT 05346
(802) 387–5566

Type of School: Co–ed boarding and day school; 137 students, grades 9–12
Tuition: $15,500 (boarding); $8,700 (day)
$ Given: $398,000 to 55 students (40% of student body)
Contact: Fred Wesson, Director of Administration

The Rock Point School
Rock Point
Burlington, VT 05401
(802) 863–1104

Type of School: Co–ed Episcopal boarding and day school; 28 students, grades 9–12
Tuition: $12,500 (boarding); $5,000 (day)
$ Given: $73,600 to 13 students (45% of student body)
Contact: Russell Ellis, Director of Administration

St. Johnsbury Academy
7 Main Street
Box B
St. Johnsbury, VT 05819
(802) 748-8171

Type of School: Co-ed boarding and day school; 794 students, grades 9-12
Tuition: $13,000 (boarding); $5,100 (day)
$ Given: $125,000 to 119 students (15% of student body)
Contact: John J. Cummings, Director of Administration

Vermont Academy
Saxtons River, VT
05154-0500
(802) 869-2121

Type of School: Co-ed boarding and day school; 250 students, grades 9-12
Tuition: $14,300 (boarding); $7,800 (day)
$ Given: $350,000 to 88 students (35% of student body)
Contact: William J. Newman, Director of Administration

VIRGINIA

Chatham Hall
Chatham, VA 24531
(804) 432-2941

Type of School: College preparatory boarding and limited day school for girls; 125 students, grades 9-12
Tuition: $15,000 (boarding); $5,000 (day)
$ Given: $210,000 to 25 students (20% of student body)
Contact: B. Bland Hotchkiss, Director of Administration

Christchurch School
Christchurch, VA 23031
(804) 758-2306

Type of School: Boys' boarding and day school; girls' day school; 255 students, grades 9-12
Tuition: $13,987 (boarding); $6,744 (day)
$ Given: $400,000 to 56 students (22% of student body)
Contact: Robert J. Murphy, Director of Administration

The Collegiate Schools
North Mooreland Road
Richmond, VA 23229
(804) 740-7077

Type of School: Co-ed; 1338 students, grades K-12
Tuition: $4,700 to $6,350
$ Given: $623,245
Contact: F. Robertson Hershey, Headmaster

The Episcopal High School
1200 N. Quaker Lane
Alexandria, VA 22302
(703) 379-6530

Type of School: Co-ed college preparatory boarding school; 284 students, grades 9-12
Tuition: $13,200
$ Given: $650,000 to 190 students (27% of student body)
Contact: John M. Walker, Jr., Director of Administration

Flint High School
10409 Academic Drive
Oakton, VA 22124
(703) 242–0705

Type of School: Co–ed day school; 425 students, grades K–12
Tuition: $7,170 to $8,455
$ Given: $304,170 to 77 students (18% of student body)
Contact: John Kennedy, Director of Administration

Foxcroft School
Middleburg, VA 22117
(703) 687–5555

Type of School: College preparatory boarding and day school for girls; 128 students, grades 9–12
Tuition: $15,000 (boarding); $8,700 (day)
$ Given: $305,000 to 31 students (24% of student body)
Contact: Rebecca B. Gilmore, Director of Administration

The Madeira School
8328 Georgetown Pike
McLean, VA 22102
(703) 556–8200

Type of School: Girls' boarding and day school; 327 students, grades 9–12
Tuition: $9,810 (day); $16,485 (boarding)
$ Given: $533,050 to 88 students (27% of student body)
Contact: M. Ellen Anderson, Director of Administration

Norfold Academy
1585 Wesleyan Drive
Norfolk, VA 23502
(804) 461–6236

Type of School: Co–ed day school; 1,168 students, grades 1–12
Tuition: $5,231 to $6,014
$ Given: $582,000 to 203 students (17% of student body)
Contact: Miriam D. Walker, Director of Administration

The Potomac School
1301 Potomac School Road
P.O. Box 430
McLean, VA 22101
(703) 356–4101

Type of School: Co–ed day school; 767 students, pre–kindergarten through grade 12
Tuition: $4,450 to $7,900
$ Given: $472,000 to 192 students (25% of student body)
Contact: Charlotte H. Nelsel, Director of Administration

St. Catherine's School
6001 Grove Avenue
Richmond, VA 23226
(804) 288–2804

Type of School: Girls' boarding (grades 9–12) and day (K–12) school
Tuition: $14,320 (boarding); $6,345 (day)
$ Given: $459,000
Contact: Auguste J. Bannard, Head of School

St. Christopher's
711 St. Christopher's Road
Richmond, VA 23226
(804) 282–3185

Type of School: Boys' day school; 790 students, junior kindergarten through grade 12
Tuition: $4,975 to $6,525
$ Given: $525,000 to 213 students (27% of student body)
Contact: George J. McVey, Headmaster

St. Stephen's and St. Agnes School Upper School
1000 St. Stephen's Road
Alexandria, VA 22304
(703) 751–2700

Type of School: 960 students, grades K–12
Tuition: $7,642 to $8,522
$ Given: $660,801 to 175 students (18% of student body)
Contact: Diane Dunning, Director of Administration

Lower and Middle Schools
400 Fontaine Street
Alexandria, VA 22302
(703) 549–3542

Type of School: 960 students, grades K–12
Tuition: $7,642 to $8,522
$ Given: $660,801 to 175 students (18% of student body)
Contact: Diane Dunning, Director of Administration

Woodberry Forest School
Woodberry Forest, VA
22989
(703) 672–3900

Type of School: College preparatory boarding and limited day school for boys; 362 students (3 in day school), grades 9–12
Tuition: $12,200 (boarding)
$ Given: $600,000 to 83 students (23% of student body)
Contact: Brendon J. O'Shea, Director of Administration

WASHINGTON

The Annie Wright School
827 N. Tacoma Avenue
Tacoma, WA 98403
(206) 272–2216

Type of School: Co–ed day school (Lower and Middle); girls' boarding and day school (Middle and Upper); 367 students
Tuition: $12,900 (boarding); $4,950 to $6,450 (day)
$ Given: $211,000 to 91 students (25% of student body)
Contact: Charles R. Griffin, Director of Administration

Epiphany School
3710 E. Howell Street
Seattle, WA 98122
(206) 323–9011

Type of School: Co–ed day school; 134 students, preschool through grade 6
Tuition: $2,772 to $4,972
$ Given: $26,473
Contact: Jean Augustine, Headmistress

Forest Ridge, A Sacred Heart School
4800 139th Avenue, SE
Bellevue, WA 98006
(206) 641–0700

Type of School: Girls' school; 240 students, grades 5–12
Tuition: $5,975 to $6,575
$ Given: $145,000 to 60 students (25% of student body)
Contact: Sister Sandra Theunick, Head of School

Lakeside School
14050 First Avenue, NE
Seattle, WA 98125
(206) 368–3600

Type of School: Co–ed; 672 students, grades 5–12
Tuition: $7,330 to $8,590
$ Given: $850,000 to 208 students (31% of student body)
Contact: A.D. Ayrault, Head of School

The Overlake School
20301 N.E. 108th
Redmond, WA 98053
(206) 868–1000

Type of School: Co–ed; 250 students, grades 6–12
Tuition: $6,700 to $7,540
$ Given: $146,000 to 58 students (23% of student body)
Contact: Joan Booms, Headmistress

Saint George's School
West 2929 Waikiki Road
Spokane, WA 99208
(509) 466–1636

Type of School: Co–ed; 250 students, kindergarten through grade 12
Tuition: $4,060 to $5,450
$ Given: $350,000 to 110 students (44% of student body)
Contact: George O. Edwards, Headmaster

University Prep
8000 25th Avenue, NE
Seattle, WA 98115
(206) 523–6407

Type of School: Co–ed; 260 students, grades 6–12
Tuition: $7,077 to $7,431
$ Given: $128,000
Contact: Roger J. Bass, Headmaster

WEST VIRGINIA

Linsly
Knox Lane
Wheeling, WV 26003
(304) 233–3260

Type of School: Co–ed boarding and day school; 390 students, grades 5–12
Tuition: $4,770 (day); $4,620 (5–day boarding); $5,300 (7–day boarding)
$ Given: $250,000 to 109 students (28% of student body)
Contact: Reno F. Di Orio, Headmaster

Wheeling Country Day School
8 Park Road
Wheeling, WV 26003
(304) 232–2430

Type of School: Co–ed; pre–kindergarten through grade 6
Tuition: $675 to $3,975
$ Given: Limited
Contact: Jesse J. Morgan, Jr., Headmaster

WISCONSIN

Brookfield Academy
3460 N. Brookfield Road
Brookfield, WI 53005
(414) 783–3200

Type of School: Co–ed day school; pre–kindergarten through grade 12
Tuition: $5,920
$ Given: $85,000
Contact: Nyle Kardatzke, President

Northwestern Military and Naval Academy
550 South Lake Shore Dr.
Lake Geneva, WI 53147
(414) 248–4465

Type of School: Episcopal boarding and day school for boys; grades 7–12
Tuition: $14,000 (boarding); $6,000 (day)
$ Given: $53,000
Contact: Col. Alfred W. Grieshaber, USAF, Superintendent

The Prairie School
4050 Lighthouse Drive
Racine, WI 53402
(414) 639–3845

Type of School: Co–ed day school; 458 students, pre–kindergarten through grade 12
Tuition: $2,100 to $4,800
$ Given: $500,000 to 215 students (47% of student body)
Contact: James B. Van Hoven, Headmaster

St. John's Military Academy
Delafield, WI 53018
(414) 646–3311

Type of School: Boys' boarding school; 208 students, grades 7–12
Tuition: $13,250
$ Given: $200,000 to 42 students (20% of student body)
Contact: LTC Gene W. Stevens, Director of Administration

University Lake School 4024 Nagawicka Road Hartland, WI 53029 (414) 367–6011	**Type of School:** Co–ed day school; 250 students, grades K–12 **Tuition:** $3,490 to $5,590 **$ Given:** $150,000 to 70 students (28% of student body) **Contact:** Richard O. Butt, Headmaster
University School of Milwaukee 2100 W. Fairy Chasm Road Milwaukee, WI 53217 (414) 352–6000	**Type of School:** Co–ed day school; 998 students, nursery through 12 **Tuition:** $2,905 to $6,520 **$ Given:** $482,000 to 126 students (13% of student body) **Contact:** John A. Stephens, Director of Administration
Wayland Academy 101–299 North University Avenue P.O. Box 398 Beaver Dam, WI 53916 (414) 885–3373	**Type of School:** Co–ed boarding and day school; 270 students, grades 9–12 **Tuition:** $13,600 (boarding); $6,200 (day) **$ Given:** $504,650 in work scholarships, endowment awards and honor scholarships to 89 students (33% of student body) **Contact:** Wendy Leigh Thompson, Dean of Administration

Miscellaneous Grants

The following chapter on "Miscellaneous Grants" lists a widely ranging array of assistance sources, such as extracurricular scholarships, religious grants and private foundation grants (including select corporate foundation sources).

Although primarily available for private school education in various religious denominations, grants also include funding to improve students' athletic skills, to support honors programs, and to support music and arts education.

As with other chapters, assistance sources are listed on a state-by-state basis. Review sources located in your state first, as much assistance of this kind is regionally based and restricted to students attending schools in specific geographic locales. Look at the funding source's specific field of interest to see if it matches your particular need or your child's area of need or expertise.

MISCELLANEOUS GRANTS

• • • • • • • • • • • • • • • • • • •

ALABAMA

Blount Foundation, Inc.
4520 Executive Park Drive
Montgomery, AL
36116–1602
(205) 244–4348

Religious Denomination: Roman Catholic, Presbyterian, Methodist, Salvation Army, United Church of Christ, Episcopal, Church of Christ, Baptist, Lutheran and nondenominational
Field of Interest: Secondary parochial education
Amount Funded: $667,434
$ Given: Ranges from $25 to $100 and from $250 to $5,000
Contact: D. Joseph McInnes, President & Director

Christian Workers Foundation
3038 Bankhead Avenue
Montgomery, AL 36106
(205) 263–5571

Religious Denomination: Nondenominational
Field of Interest: Secondary parochial education
Amount Funded: $115,000
$ Given: $1,000 to $10,000
Contact: Allen W. Mathis, Jr., Trustee

The Sonat Foundation, Inc.
1900 Fifth Avenue, North
P.O. Box 2563
Birmingham, AL 35203
(205) 325–7460

Description: Scholarships to children of employees of Sonat, Inc.
$ Given: $88,750 in grants to 37 individuals
Application Procedure: Initial approach by letter; applications accepted throughout the year
Contact: Darlene Sanders, Secretary

ALASKA

CIRI Foundation
a/k/a The Cook Inlet Region, Inc. Foundation
P.O. Box 93330
Anchorage, AK 99509–3330
(907) 274–8638

Description: Grants to individuals for educational support of enrollees of Cook Inlet Region; given also for native cultural and heritage products
$ Given: $150 to $5,000 in student aid, grants to individuals, internships, fellowships and special projects
Requirements: Applicant must be an enrollee or child or spouse of an enrollee of Cook Inlet Region for individual education scholarship grants

ARIZONA

Tell Foundation
4020 North 38th Avenue
Phoenix, AZ 85019
(602) 278–6209

Religious Denomination: Christian
Field of Interest: Elementary and secondary parochial education
Amount Funded: $115,231
$ Given: $500 to $3,500
Contact: Ronald L. Lewis, Foundation Administrator

ARKANSAS

Sturgis (Roy & Christine) Charitable & Educational Trust
P.O. Box 92
Malvern, AR 72104
(501) 332–3899

Religious Denomination: Baptist and Roman Catholic
Field of Interest: Elementary parochial education

Tyson Foundation, Inc.
P.O. Drawer E
Springdale, AR 72764
(501) 756–4513

Description: Grants for community projects, education, social services and culture; scholarships and student aid also available to individuals; giving limited to the mid–South area
$ Given: $96,230 in grants to individuals
Application Procedure: Completion of formal application required
Contact: Oleta Selman

CALIFORNIA

Amado Foundation
3600 Wilshire Boulevard, Suite 1228
Los Angeles, CA 90010
(213) 381–3632

Religious Denomination: Jewish
Field of Interest: Primary and secondary education
Contact: Stella A. Lavis, President

MISCELLANEOUS GRANTS

American Honda Foundation
P.O. Box 2205
700 Van Ness Avenue
Torrance, CA 90509–2205
(213) 781–4090

Description: Funds to continue the American Honda Foundation Individual Honors Program for 7th and 8th graders at Walter Reed Junior High School, North Hollywood, California
$ Given: $25,000
Contact: Amy Tone or Donna Hammond

Blues Heaven Foundation
c/o The Cameron Organization, Inc.
2001 W. Magnolia, Suite E
Burbank, CA 91506–1704
(818) 566–8880

Field of Interest: Music education
Description: Muddy Waters scholarship fund for students seeking music education; assistance to elementary, secondary and high schools in obtaining musical instruments
Contact: Willie Dixon, President & Founder

Burns–Dunphy Foundation
Hearst Building, Suite 1200
Third and Market Streets
San Francisco, CA 94103
(415) 421–6995

Religious Denomination: Roman Catholic, Episcopal, United Methodist, Jewish, Salvation Army
Field of Interest: Primary education
Contact: Walter M. Gleason

Clougherty (Francis H.) Charitable Trust
P.O. Box 93490
Pasadena, CA 91109
(818) 793–1163

Religious Denomination: Roman Catholic
Field of Interest: Elementary and secondary parochial education
Contact: Joseph D. Clougherty, Trustee

Cross Examination Debate Association
Department of Speech
California State University, Northridge
Northridge, CA 91330
(818) 885–2633

Field of Interest: Debate
Contact: Don Brownlee, Executive Secretary

Diener (Frank C.) Foundation
P.O. Box 278
Five Points, CA 93624
(209) 224–9112

Religious Denomination: Roman Catholic
Field of Interest: Secondary parochial education
Amount Funded: $82,250
$ Given: $2,000 to $10,000
Contact: Mary Alice Diener, President

Doheny (Carrie Estelle) Foundation
1010 S. Flower St., Ste. 400
Los Angeles, CA 90015
(213) 748–5111

Religious Denomination: Roman Catholic, nondenominational and Salvation Army
Field of Interest: Secondary parochial education
Contact: Robert A. Smith, Jr., President

Friedman Brothers Foundation
801 E. Commercial Street
Los Angeles, CA 90012

Religious Denomination: Jewish
Description: Emphasis on education, including religious education and Jewish religious & welfare organizations
$ Given: $1,000 to $40,000
Application Procedure: Write to 184 Sherwood Place, Englewood, NJ 07631

Gallo (Julio R.) Foundation
P.O. Box 1130
Modesto, CA 95353
(209) 579–3373

Religious Denomination: Roman Catholic
Field of Interest: Elementary and secondary parochial education
Amount Funded: $192,500
Contact: Robert J. Gallo, Vice President

Gellert (Carl) Foundation
2222 Nineteenth Avenue
San Francisco, CA 94116
(415) 566–4420

Religious Denomination: Christian, Episcopal, Lutheran, Roman Catholic
Field of Interest: Elementary and secondary parochial education
Contact: Peter J. Brusati, Secretary

Hayden (William R. & Virginia) Foundation
110 W. Las Tunas Drive, Suite A
San Gabriel, CA 91776
(818) 285–9891

Religious Denomination: Roman Catholic
Field of Interest: Elementary and secondary parochial education

Hinz Family Charitable Foundation
c/o Hi Torque Publications
10600 Sepulveda
Mission Hills, CA 91345
(818) 365–6831

Religious Denomination: Congregational Christian Church and nondenominational
Field of Interest: Elementary parochial education
Amount Funded: $650,150
$ Given: $4,000 to $60,000
Contact: Roland Hinz, Trustee

Jameson (J.W. & Ida M.) Foundation
P.O. Box 397
Sierra Madre, CA 91024–0397
(818) 355–6973

Religious Denomination: Episcopal, Lutheran, Roman Catholic, Baptist, and Salvation Army
Field of Interest: Secondary parochial education
Amount Funded: $619,000
$ Given: $2,500 to $10,000
Contact: Arthur W. Kirk, President

Leavy (Thomas & Dorothy) Foundation
4680 Wilshire Boulevard
Los Angeles, CA 90010
(213) 930–4252

Religious Denomination: Roman Catholic and Protestant
Field of Interest: Elementary and secondary parochial education
Contact: J. Thomas McCarthy, President

Leonart Foundation
1801 Avenue of the Stars
Suite 811
Los Angeles, CA 90067
(213) 556–3932

Religious Denomination: Roman Catholic
Field of Interest: Secondary parochial education
Contact: Felix McGinnis, Jr., President

Lund Foundation
P.O. Box 15159
North Hollywood, CA 91615

Description: Grants for the arts and education, including secondary education
$ Given: $50,042 to eight individuals (low-end grant about $1,048)

Marini Family Trust
c/o Wells Fargo Bank
MAC–0101–056
420 Montgomery Street
San Francisco, CA 94163
(415) 396–2923

Religious Denomination: Roman Catholic and Salvation Army
Field of Interest: Secondary parochial education
Amount Funded: $184,986
$ Given: $1,000 to $10,000
Contact: Eugene J. Rhangiasci, Trust Officer

Menlo Foundation
501 S. Fairfax Avenue
Los Angeles, CA 90036

Religious Denomination: Jewish
Description: Awards to Jewish organizations, including educational institutions
Contact: Sam Menlo, Trustee

Murphy (Dan) Foundation
P.O. Box 711267
Los Angeles, CA 90071
(213) 623–3120

Religious Denomination: Roman Catholic
Field of Interest: Secondary education
Amount Funded: $4,349,139
$ Given: $1,000 to $25,000
Contact: Grace Robinson, Secretary

National Hispanic Scholarship Fund
P.O. Box 748
San Francisco, CA 94101

Description: Scholarships to Hispanic–American undergraduate and graduate students
Amount Funded: $2,000,000
Contact: Ernest Z. Robles, Executive Director

National Scholastic Surfing Association
P.O. Box 495
Huntington Beach, CA 92648
(714) 841–3254

Description: Scholarships to outstanding student surfers, grade 6 through college
Contact: Carolyn Adams, Executive Director

Stulsaft (Morris) Foundation
100 Bush Street
San Francisco, CA 94101
(415) 986–7117

Religious Denomination: Christian, Jewish
Field of Interest: Parochial education
Application Procedure: apply by letter to Susan Mora (6–7 month waiting period)
Contact: Joan Nelson Dills, Administrator

Sundean Foundation
927 Hanover Street
Santa Cruz, CA 95060
(408) 425–5927

Religious Denomination: Adventist and nondenominational
Field of Interest: Elementary and secondary parochial education
Amount Funded: $443,532
$ Given: Ranges from $100 to $1,000 and from $10,000 to $50,000
Contact: Harold A. Sundean, President

Trust Funds, Inc.
100 Broadway, Third Floor
San Francisco, CA 94111
(415) 434–3323

Religious Denomination: Roman Catholic
Field of Interest: Secondary parochial education
Contact: Albert J. Steiss, President

COLORADO

United States Swimming, Inc.
1750 E. Boulder Street
Colorado Springs, CO 80909
(719) 578–4578

Description: Swimming programs for persons 5 years and older; awards to swimmers and volunteers
Amount Funded: $4,800,000
Contact: Ray B. Essick, Executive Director

Weckbaugh (Eleanore Mullen) Foundation
P.O. Box 31678
Aurora, CO 80041
(303) 367–1545

Religious Denomination: Roman Catholic and Jewish
Field of Interest: Elementary and secondary parochial education
Contact: Edward J. Limes

William & Laura Younger Memorial Fund
354 Cherry Street
Denver, CO 80220
(303) 333–8126

Religious Denomination: Jewish
Description: Grants and loans for scholarships restricted to needy and qualified Jewish children seeking an education
Amount Funded: $6,000
$ Given: One annual grant to an individual, in the amount of $6,000
Contact: Hyman A. Coggan

CONNECTICUT

Army Aviation Association of America
49 Richmondville Avenue
Westport, CT 06880
(203) 226–8184

Description: Scholarships to children and spouses of members
Contact: Terrence M. Coakley, Executive Director

Lender Family Foundation, Inc.
1764 Litchfield Turnpike
Woodbridge, CT 06525
(203) 397–3977

Religious Denomination: Jewish
Field of Interest: Elementary and secondary parochial education
Contact: April Saba, Secretary

Panwy Foundation
P.O. Box 1800
Greenwich, CT 06836
(203) 661–6616

Religious Denomination: Protestant, Roman Catholic and Jewish
Field of Interest: Secondary parochial education
Amount Funded: $320,945
$ Given: $25 to $5,000
Contact: Ralph M. Wyman, President

Trachten (Morris & Sylvia) Family Foundation
33–39 John Street
New Britain, CT 06051
(203) 225–6478

Religious Denomination: Jewish
Field of Interest: Elementary and secondary parochial education
Amount Funded: $151,788
Contact: Morris Trachten, Trustee

MISCELLANEOUS GRANTS

. . . .

DELAWARE

Misses Hebb Memorial Fund
c/o Bank of Delaware
300 Delaware Avenue
Wilmington, DE 19801

Description: Scholarships for secondary education to students at the Tatnall School, Wilmington, Delaware
$ Given: One grant for $3,103 awarded
Application Procedure: Applications accepted throughout the year

Raskob Foundation for Catholic Activities, Inc.
P.O. Box 4019
Wilmington, DE 19807
(302) 655–4440

Religious Denomination: Roman Catholic
Field of Interest: Elementary and secondary parochial education
Amount Funded: $2,879,026
$ Given: $100 to $100,000
Contact: Gerard S. Garey, President

DISTRICT OF COLUMBIA

Gudelsky (Isadore & Bertha) Family Foundation
1503 21st Street, NW
Washington, DC 20036
(202) 328–0500

Religious Denomination: Jewish
Field of Interest: Elementary and secondary parochial education
Amount Funded: $704,667
$ Given: $5,000 to $20,000
Contact: Philip N. Margolius

Mathematical Association of America
1529 18th Street, NW
Washington, DC 20036
(202) 389–5200

Description: Annual high school mathematics contests
Contact: Marcia P. Sward, Executive Director

FLORIDA

Bastien (John E. & Nellie J.) Memorial Foundation
6991 West Broward Blvd.
Fort Lauderdale, FL 33317
(305) 791–0810

Religious Denomination: Roman Catholic, Lutheran, Baptist, Jewish, Methodist, and Presbyterian
Field of Interest: Primary education
Contact: J. Wallace Wrightson, Trustee

Saint Gerard Foundation
3041 Braeloch Circle East
Clearwater, FL 34021–2708

Religious Denomination: Roman Catholic, United Methodist, Salvation Army
Field of Interest: Parochial education
Contact: Elizabeth C. Mooney, Vice President

GEORGIA

Patterson–Barclay Memorial Foundation, Inc.
P.O. 7370 Station C
Atlanta, GA 30357
(404) 876–1022

Religious Denomination: Jewish, Protestant and Roman Catholic
Field of Interest: Secondary parochial education
Amount Funded: $251,500
$ Given: $1,000 to $5,000
Contact: Lee Patterson Allen, Trustee

Rainbow Fund
P.O. Box 937
Fort Valley, GA 31030
(912) 825–2021

Religious Denomination: Evangelical, interdenominational, nondenominational, Protestant and Roman Catholic
Field of Interest: Secondary parochial education
Amount Funded: $1,483,199
$ Given: $250 to $5,000
Contact: George Luce, Chairman

HAWAII

Atherton Family Foundation
c/o Hawaiian Community Foundation
212 Merchant St., Suite 330
Honolulu, HI 96813
(808) 536–7290

Religious Denomination: All
Field of Interest: Secondary education
Contact: Jane R. Smith, Secretary

ILLINOIS

Bowyer Foundation
175 West Jackson Boulevard, Suite 909
Chicago, IL 60604
(312) 427–6339

Religious Denomination: Roman Catholic
Field of Interest: Primary education
Contact: David T. Hutchinson, President

MISCELLANEOUS GRANTS

• • • • • • • • • • • • • • • • • • •

Chernin's Shoes Foundation
Attn: Steven B. Larrick
1001 South Clinton Street
Chicago, IL 60607
(312) 922-5900

Religious Denomination: Jewish, Church of God, Roman Catholic and Methodist
Field of Interest: Secondary parochial education
Amount Funded: $108,303
$ Given: Ranges from $100 to $500 and from $1,000 to $10,000

Christian Evangelical Foundation
c/o Lustick, Huizenga & Williams, Ltd.
20 N. Wacker Dr., Ste. 2800
Chicago, IL 60606
(312) 372-1033

Religious Denomination: Presbyterian, Christian, Evangelical, nondenominational
Field of Interest: Primary and secondary education
Contact: Jack Lustick, Council

Louis (Michael W.) Foundation
2840 Sheridan Road
Evanston, IL 60201
(312) 256-5150

Religious Denomination: Presbyterian, Roman Catholic, and United Methodist
Field of Interest: Elementary and secondary parochial education
Amount Funded: $1,738,225
$ Given: $700 to $6,000
Contact: Orley R. Herron, President

National Interscholastic Swimming Coaches Association of America
Glenbrook South High School
4000 W. Lake Avenue
Glenview, IL 60025
(708) 729-2000

Field of Interest: Aquatics
Description: Awards and programs for intermediate and secondary school students to improve and advance aquatics skills
Contact: Donald R. Allen

Schmitt (Arthur J.) Foundation
Two North LaSalle Street
Suite 2010
Chicago, IL 60602
(312) 236-5089

Religious Denomination: Roman Catholic
Field of Interest: Elementary and secondary parochial education
Amount Funded: $1,111,600
$ Given: $1,000 to $5,000
Contact: John A. Donahue, Executive Secretary

Snite (Fred B.) Foundation
550 Frontage Rd., No. 3082
Northfield, IL 60093
(312) 446–7705

Religious Denomination: Roman Catholic and Episcopal
Field of Interest: Elementary and secondary parochial education
Amount Funded: $288,800
$ Given: $1,000 to $10,000
Contact: Terrence J. Dillon, President & Director

Solo Cup Foundation
1700 Old Deerfield Road
Highland Park, IL 60035
(312) 831–4800

Religious Denomination: Roman Catholic
Field of Interest: Elementary and secondary parochial education
Amount Funded: $240,700
$ Given: $5,000 to $10,000
Contact: Ron Whaley, Director

State Farm Companies Foundation
One State Farm Plaza
Bloomington, IL 61710
(309) 766–2039

Description: Scholarships to children of State Farm employees or agents
$ Given: $297,773 in grants to individuals
Application Procedure: Deadline December 31; completion of formal application required
Contact: Dave Polzin, Assistant Program Vice President

Ven Der Molen (Everett & Joyce) Foundation
IN 335 Indian Knoll Road
West Chicago, IL 60185
(312) 876–0100

Religious Denomination: Christian Reformed Church and Presbyterian
Field of Interest: Secondary parochial education
Amount Funded: $182,876
$ Given: Ranges from $100 to $500 and from $1,000 to $20,000
Contact: Everett R. Van Der Molen, Director

White (W.P. & H.B.) Foundation
540 Frontage Rd., Ste. 332
Northfield, IL 60093
(312) 446–1441

Religious Denomination: Nondenominational and Roman Catholic
Field of Interest: Secondary parochial education
Amount Funded: $839,350
$ Given: $2,000 to $8,000
Contact: John H. McCortney, Treasurer

MISCELLANEOUS GRANTS

. . . .

INDIANA

Christian Foundation
301 Washington Street
P.O. Box 808
Columbus, IN 47202
(812) 376–3331

Religious Denomination: Church of Christ
Amount Funded: $1,085,530
Contact: Owen D. Hungerford, Secretary

Council for National Cooperation in Aquatics
901 W. New York Street
Indianapolis, IN 46223
(317) 638–4238

Field of Interest: Aquatics
Description: National Advisory Committee on Aquatics for Young Children sponsors scholarship program
Contact: Louise Priest, Executive Director

Hillenbrand (John A.) Foundation, Inc.
Highway 46
Batesville, IN 47006
(812) 934–7000

Religious Denomination: Roman Catholic, Pentecostal, Baptist, Church of Christ, United Methodist, Latter Day Saints, and Lutheran
Field of Interest: Secondary parochial education
Amount Funded: $167,004
$ Given: $1,500 to $5,000
Contact: Daniel A. Hillenbrand, President

Murphy College Fund
c/o First National Bank
of Warsaw
Trust Department
P.O. Box 1447
Warsaw, IN 46580

Description: Scholarships only to residents of Kosciusko County, IN, or graduates of Kosciusko County School; awards made to individuals in the fields of music education, church ministries, physical therapy, secondary education, computer programming, nursing, Spanish language education, and engineering; some preference given to students entering a medical field of any kind
Amount Funded: $4,145
$ Given: Seven grants to individuals, ranging from $375 to $750

United States Gymnastics Federation
201 S. Capitol, Suite 300
Indianapolis, IN 46225
(317) 237–5050

Field of Interest: Gymnastics
Amount Funded: $7,500,000
Contact: Mike Jacki, Executive Director

IOWA

Blank (Myron & Jaqueline) Charity Fund
Insurance Exchange Bldg.
505 Fifth Avenue, Suite 414
Des Moines, IA 50309
(515) 243–5287

Religious Denomination: Jewish, United Methodist, Roman Catholic, and nondenominational
Field of Interest: Primary education
Contact: Myron N. Blank, President/Treasurer/Director

Pritchard Educational Fund
c/o Cherokee State Bank
212 West Willow Street
Cherokee, IA 51012
(712) 225–5131

Description: Student loans for residents of Cherokee County, Iowa, for high school or college education expenses
Amount Funded: $98,950 in loans
$ Given: $300 to $1,000 per loan; to 148 individuals
Contact: Leon Klotz, Foundation Manager

Vermeer Foundation
c/o Vermeer Manufacturing Co.
Box 200
Pella, IA 50219
(515) 628–3141

Religious Denomination: Christian, Evangelical, United Methodist, and Baptist
Field of Interest: Secondary education
Amount Funded: $1,101,638
$ Given: Ranges from $250 to $5,000 and from $10,000 to $50,000
Contact: Lois Vermeer, Secretary & Director

Vermeer Charitable Foundation, Inc.
c/o Vermeer Manufacturing Co.
Box 200
Pella, IA 50219
(515) 628–3141

Religious Denomination: Christian and nondenominational
Field of Interest: Elementary and secondary parochial education
Amount Funded: $293,997
$ Given: $1,000 to $10,000
Contact: Mary Andringa, Director

LOUISIANA

Lupin Foundation
3715 Prytania Street
Suite 403
New Orleans, LA 70115
(504) 897–6125

Religious Denomination: Episcopal, Jewish and Roman Catholic
Field of Interest: Secondary parochial education
Amount Funded: $834,512
$ Given: $1,000 to $25,000
Contact: Lori Strahan, Program Coordinator

MISCELLANEOUS GRANTS

• • • • • • • • • • • • • • • • • • •

MARYLAND

Hoffberger Foundation
900 Garrett Building
233 E. Redwood Street
Baltimore, MD 21202
(301) 576–4205

Religious Denomination: Jewish
Field of Interest: Secondary parochial education
Amount Funded: $305,500
$ Given: $1,000 to $2,500
Contact: LeRoy Edward Hoffberger, President

Knott (Marion I. & Henry J.) Foundation, Inc.
3904 Hickory Avenue
Baltimore, MD 21211
(301) 235–7068

Religious Denomination: Roman Catholic
Field of Interest: Elementary and secondary parochial education
Contact: Ann von Lossberg, Administrator

Mary Byrd Wyman Memorial Association of Baltimore City
3130 Golf Course Road West
Owings Mills, MD 21117

Description: Scholarships for secondary education
Amount Funded: $42,000
$ Given: $1,300 to $2,000 per grant; to 27 individuals
Application Procedure: Deadline January 1
Contact: A. Rutherford Holmes, President

MASSACHUSETTS

Birmingham Foundation
2743 Wormwood Street
Boston, MA 02210
(617) 723–7430

Religious Denomination: Roman Catholic
Field of Interest: Primary and secondary education
Application Procedure: Submit application before end of third quarter of each calendar year
Contact: Barbara Burke

The Boston Globe Foundation, Inc.
c/o The Boston Globe
135 William T. Morrissey Boulevard
Boston, MA 02107
(617) 929–2895

Description: Scholarships to employees of Affiliated Publications, Inc. and its subsidiaries, their families, and residents in the area of company operations of metropolitan Boston
Amount Funded: $1,198,424
$ Given: 14 grants to individuals, totalling $15,927 and ranging from $77 to $2,500
Contact: Suzanne T. Watkin, Executive Director

Fireman (Paul & Phyllis) Charitable Foundation
P.O. Box 9145
Canton, MA 02021
(617) 821–2800

Religious Denomination: Jewish and United Methodist
Field of Interest: Secondary parochial education
Amount Funded: $1,211,700
$ Given: Ranges from $250 to $3,500 and from $20,000 to $550,000
Contact: Phyllis Fireman, Trust

Melville (David B.) Foundation
30 Colpitts Road
Weston, MA 02193
(617) 891–7755

Religious Denomination: Christian and Baptist
Field of Interest: Secondary parochial education
Contact: E. Christopher Palmer, Trustee

Walsh (Blanch M.) Trust
174 Central Street
Lowell, MA 01852
(617) 454–5654

Religious Denomination: Roman Catholic
Field of Interest: Elementary and secondary parochial education
Amount Funded: $159,550
$ Given: $750 to $5,500
Contact: Robert F. Murphy, Jr., Trustee

MICHIGAN

Bargman (Theodore & Mina) Foundation
29201 Telegraph Rd., Ste. 500
Southfield, MI 48034
(313) 358–9500

Religious Denomination: Jewish
Field of Interest: Parochial education
Contact: Lawrence Jackier, President & Trustee

DeVos (Richard & Helen) Foundation
7575 E. Fulton Road
Ada, MI 49355
(616) 676–6753

Religious Denomination: Christian
Field of Interest: Secondary parochial education
Contact: Richard DeVos, President

Evereg–Fenesse Mesrobian–Roupenian Educational Society, Inc.
P.O. Box 463
Lathrop Village, MI 48076

Description: Scholarships to students attending Armenian day schools
$ Given: $1,000 to $2,650
Application Procedure: Deadline December 15; completion of formal application required; standard application forms available for designated representatives
Contact: Rose Boudakian

Honigman Foundation, Inc.
2290 First National Bldg.
Detroit, MI 48226
(313) 256–7500

Religious Denomination: Jewish
Field of Interest: Secondary parochial education
Amount Funded: $177,984
$ Given: Ranges from $50 to $500 and from $1,000 to $10,000
Contact: Jason L. Honigman, President

Michner (Joseph & Lottie) Education Foundation
P.O. Box 785
Jackson, MI 49204
(517) 787–6130

Description: Scholarships for 3–5 students to attend Lumen Christi High School, Jackson, Michigan
$ Given: Three grants totalling $3,900; each grant for $1,300

Sage Foundation
150 W. Jefferson, Ste. 2500
Detroit, MI 48226
(313) 963–6420

Religious Denomination: Nondenominational
Field of Interest: Elementary and secondary parochial education
Amount Funded: $2,213,675
$ Given: $2,000 to $15,000
Contact: Melissa Sage Booth, President

Van Andel (Jay & Betty) Foundation
7186 Windy Hill Road, SE
Grand Rapids, MI 49546
(616) 676–6000

Religious Denomination: Christian, nondenominational, Evangelical, Baptist, Presbyterian, and Salvation Army
Field of Interest: Elementary and secondary parochial education
Amount Funded: $610,410
$ Given: $1,000 to $10,000
Contact: Jay Van Andel, President

MINNESOTA

Butler (Patrick & Aimee) Foundation
E–1420 First National Bank Building
St. Paul, MN 55101
(612) 222–2565

Religious Denomination: Roman Catholic, nondenominational, Salvation Army, and United Church of Christ
Field of Interest: Secondary parochial education
Amount Funded: $652,750
$ Given: $1,000 to $25,000
Contact: Sandra Butler, Program Officer

O'Neil (Casey Albert T.) Foundation
c/o First Trust Company, Inc.
W–555 First National Bank Building
St. Paul, MN 44101
(612) 291–5114

Religious Denomination: Roman Catholic and nondenominational
Field of Interest: Secondary parochial education
Amount Funded: $686,500
$ Given: $2,500 to $30,000
Contact: Jeffrey T. Peterson

O'Shaughnessy (I.A.) Foundation, Inc.
P.O. Box 64704
First Trust National Assn.
St. Paul, MN 55164
(612) 223–7509

Religious Denomination: Roman Catholic and Methodist
Field of Interest: Secondary parochial education
Amount Funded: $1,895,110
$ Given: $5,000 to $50,000
Contact: Rodney Thain, Trust Officer

Quinlan (Elizabeth C.) Foundation, Inc.
1205 Foshay Tower
Minneapolis, MN 55402
(612) 333–8084

Religious Denomination: Eastern churches and Roman Catnolic
Field of Interest: Secondary parochial education
Amount Funded: $297,041
Contact: Kathy Iverson

MISSISSIPPI

Walker (W.E.) Foundation
1675 Lakeland Drive
Riverhill Tower, Suite 400
Jackson, MS 39216
(601) 362–9895

Religious Denomination: Episcopal, Presbyterian, and Pentecostal
Field of Interest: Secondary parochial education
Amount Funded: $238,922
$ Given: Ranges from $200 to $1,000, and $2,000 to $10,000
Contact: W.E. Walker, Jr., Trustee

MISSOURI

Gaylord (Catherine Manley) Foundation
314 N. Broadway,
Suite 1230
St. Louis, MO 63102
(314) 421–0181

Religious Denomination: Methodist, Episcopal, Roman Catholic, Presbyterian, Unitarian Universalist, and Church of God
Field of Interest: Elementary and secondary parochial education
Amount Funded: $261,800
$ Given: $1,000 to $23,000
Contact: Donald E. Fahey, Trustee

Orscheln Industries Foundation, Inc.
P.O. Box 698
Moberly, MO 65270
(816) 263–4335

Religious Denomination: Roman Catholic, Christian, Presbyterian, Baptist, Lutheran, Salvation Army, Mennonite, and nondenominational
Field of Interest: Elementary and secondary parochial education
Amount Funded: $644,490
$ Given: $1,000 to $10,000
Contact: J.H. Hartley, Foundation Representative

Pendergast–Weyer Foundation
P.O. Box 413245
Kansas City, MO 64141
(816) 561–6340

Religious Denomination: Roman Catholic and Presbyterian
Field of Interest: Elementary and secondary parochial education
Amount Funded: $140,000
$ Given: $5,000 to $25,000
Contact: Thomas J. Pendergast, Jr., President & Director

Sycamore Tree Trust
7733 Forsyth Boulevard
Suite 1050
St. Louis, MO 63105
(314) 725–8666

Religious Denomination: Roman Catholic
Field of Interest: Elementary and secondary parochial education
Contact: Joseph C. Morris, Vice President

Voelkerding (Walter & Jean) Charitable Trust
P.O. Box 81
Dutzow, MO 63342
(314) 433–5520

Religious Denomination: Roman Catholic, Lutheran, and United Church of Christ
Field of Interest: Secondary parochial education
Amount Funded: $68,000
$ Given: $5,000 to $8,000

NEVADA

Rochlin (Abraham & Sarah) Foundation
275 Hill Street, No. 25
Reno, NV 89501
(702) 827–3550

Religious Denomination: Jewish
Field of Interest: Elementary and secondary parochial education
Amount Funded: $1,266,726
Contact: Larry Rochlin, President

NEW JERSEY

Bendheim (Charles & Els) Foundation
One Parker Plaza
Fort Lee, NJ 07024

Description: Grants to Jewish individuals for religious studies

Brennan (Robert E.) Foundation
c/o Mortenson, Fleming et. al.
340 North Avenue
Cranford, NJ 07016
(201) 272–7000

Religious Denomination: Roman Catholic
Field of Interest: Secondary parochial education

Grassmann (E.J.) Trust
P.O. Box 4470
Warren, NJ 07060
(201) 753–2440

Religious Denomination: Nondenominational, Roman Catholic, Baptist, and United Methodist
Field of Interest: Secondary parochial education
Contact: William V. Engel, Executive Director

Hackett Foundation
33 Second Street
Raritan, NJ 08869
(201) 231–8252

Religious Denomination: Roman Catholic
Field of Interest: Secondary parochial education
Contact: Alice T. Hackett

National Junior Tennis League
USTA Center for Education
& Recreational Tennis
707 Alexander Road
Princeton, NJ 08540
(609) 452–2580

Description: Scholarships and programs in children's tennis

Taub (Henry & Marilyn) Foundation
354 Eisenhower Parkway
Livingston, NJ 07039
(201) 994–9400

Religious Denomination: Jewish
Field of Interest: Elementary and secondary parochial education
Contact: Mildred Feldstein

The Wight Foundation, Inc.
189 Mill Road
Saddle River, NJ 07458

Description: Scholarships for high school education, primarily boarding school
Amount Funded: $241,831
$ Given: Awards ranging from $4,325 to $20,943 ($7,000 average), to 29 individuals
Application Procedure: Names submitted to foundation for var-ious private schools; direct applications for students not accepted
Contact: Russell Wight, Jr., President

NEW YORK

American Friends of the Paris Opera and Ballet
972 Fifth Avenue
New York, NY 10021
(212) 439–1400

Field of Interest: Opera and ballet
Description: Scholarships to U.S. students and performers
Contact: Michael David–Weill, Board Chairman

Baird Foundation
P.O. Box 514
Williamsville, NY 14221
(716) 633–5588

Religious Denomination: Roman Catholic, Episcopal, and Congregational Christian Church
Field of Interest: Secondary education
Amount Funded: $1,642,916
$ Given: $1,000 to $2,000
Contact: Carl E. Gruber, Manager

Bnei Akiva of North America
25 West 26th Street
New York, NY 10010
(212) 889–5260

Religious Denomination: Jewish/Zionist
Description: Sponsor of Bnei Akiva Scholarship Institute for boys and girls (aged 10–18) in Zionist youth movement
Amount Funded: $250,000
Contact: Noon Slomowitz, Executive Officer

Boces Geneseo Migrant Center
Holcomb 210–211
Geneseo, NY 14454
(716) 245–5681

Description: Scholarship awards from the Gloria & Joseph Mattena National Scholarship Fund for Migrant Children to enable migrant youth to remain in school

Booth Ferris Foundation
30 Broad Street
New York, NY 10040
(212) 269–3850

Religious Denomination: Roman Catholic, Baptist, nondenominational, Presbyterian, Episcopal, Jewish, Buddhist, and Church of Christ
Field of Interest: Secondary parochial education
Amount Funded: $4,893,434
$ Given: $25,000 to $100,000
Contact: Robert J. Murtagh, Trustee

Brecher Fund
48 Concord Drive
Monsey, NY 10952
(914) 352–0498

Religious Denomination: Jewish
Field of Interest: Primary and secondary education
Contact: Harvey Brecher, Director

Brothers Ashkenazi Foundation
445 Park Avenue
New York, NY 10022
(212) 434–1050

Religious Denomination: Jewish
Field of Interest: Secondary parochial education
Amount Funded: $1,221,808
$ Given: $100 to $10,000
Contact: Ely E. Ashkenazi, President

MISCELLANEOUS GRANTS

Brunner (Robert) Foundation
c/o Capramont Ltd.
63 Wall Street, Suite 1903
New York, NY 10005
(212) 344–0050

Religious Denomination: Roman Catholic
Field of Interest: Primary and secondary education
Contact: John M. Bruderman, Jr.

Carnegie Corporation of New York
Education and Health Development of Children and Youth
437 Madison Avenue
New York, NY 10022

Description: Focus on children and youth to age 15; concentration on early childhood, early adolescence, science education, and education reform.
Contact: Dorothy Knapp, Secretary

Delany (Beatrice P.) Charitable Trust
Chase Manhattan Bank N.A.
1211 Avenue of the Americas
New York, NY 10036
(212) 730–3885

Religious Denomination: Nondenominational
Field of Interest: Secondary parochial education
Contact: Harry S. Stotter, Vice President

Elenberg (Charles and Anna) Foundation, Inc.
c/o Jack Scharf
P.O. Box 630193
Spuyten Duyvil Station
Bronx, NY 10463
(718) 769–8728

Religious Denomination: Jewish
Description: Scholarships to needy students of Hebrew faith who are attending high school or college, with preference given to orphans; no grants to married students
Amount Funded: $44,075
$ Given: 283 grants to individuals
Application Procedure: For guidelines, write to 3133 Brighton Seventh Street, Brooklyn, NY 11235
Contact: Rabbi David B. Hollander

Fischel (Harry & Jane) Foundation
310 Madison Ave., Ste. 1711
New York, NY 10001
(212) 599–2828

Religious Denomination: Jewish
Field of Interest: Parochial education
Contact: Michael D. Jaspan, Executive Director

Gordon Fund
20 Exchange Place, 8th Fl.
New York, NY 10005
(212) 510–5311

Religious Denomination: Episcopal and Roman Catholic
Field of Interest: Elementary and secondary parochial education
Amount Funded: $1,245,250
$ Given: $1,000 to $30,000
Contact: William N. Loverd, Trustee

The James Gordon Bennett Memorial Corporation
c/o New York Daily News
220 East 42nd Street
New York, NY 10017

Description: Scholarships to children of journalists who have worked in New York City on daily newspapers for ten years or more
Amount Funded: $162,563
$ Given: 151 scholarships ranging from $250 to $3,250; remainder of grants to individuals totals $71,415
Contact: Denise Houserman

Katzenberger Foundation
6 East 43rd Street
New York, NY 10017
(212) 687–3340

Religious Denomination: Church of Christ, Scientist
Field of Interest: Secondary parochial education
Amount Funded: $500,000
$ Given: $1,000 to $5,000
Contact: Abner J. Golieb, President

Link (George), Jr. Foundation
c/o Emmet, Marvin and Martin
48 Wall Street
New York, NY 10005
(212) 422–2974

Religious Denomination: Roman Catholic
Field of Interest: Secondary parochial education
Contact: Michael J. Catanzaro, Vice President

O'Toole (Theresa & Edward) Foundation, Inc.
Bank of New York Trust Department
48 Wall Street
New York, NY 10015
(212) 449–1183

Religious Denomination: Roman Catholic
Field of Interest: Elementary and secondary parochial education
Amount Funded: $704,482
$ Given: $1,000 to $10,000
Contact: Dan McCarthy, Trust Officer

MISCELLANEOUS GRANTS

• • • • • • • • • • • • • • • • • • •

Rosenberg (Sunny & Abe) Foundation, Inc.
c/o Robert Gassman
350 Fifth Avenue
New York, NY 10118
(212) 239–1280

Religious Denomination: Jewish, Salvation Army, and Protestant
Field of Interest: Secondary parochial education
Contact: Sonia Rosenberg, Vice President & Secretary

Rosenblum (Sanford & Dina) Foundation
732 Madison Avenue
Albany, NY 12208
(518) 463–1107

Religious Denomination: Jewish
Field of Interest: Elementary and secondary parochial education
Amount Funded: $91,420
$ Given: $2,000 to $20,000
Contact: Sanford Rosenblum, Director

Stein (Joseph F.) Foundation
28 Aspen Road
Scarsdale, NY 10583
(914) 725–1770

Religious Denomination: Jewish
Field of Interest: Elementary and secondary parochial education
Amount Funded: $560,081
$ Given: $100 to $10,000
Contact: Melvin M. Stein, Manager

Teamsters BBYO Scholarship Fund
22 Park Avenue South
New York, NY 10003
(212) 254–8424

Description: Grants for individuals in the Northeast region to attend B'nai Brith Youth Organization Summer Program
$ Given: $250 to $2,000
Application Procedure: Deadline March 20; completion of formal application required
Contact: Martin Adelstein or nearest B'nai Brith

Violin Society of America
85–07 Abingdon Road
Kew Gardens, NY 11415
(718) 849–1373

Field of Interest: Musical instrument production/restoration
Description: Kaplan–Goodkind Memorial Scholarship for worthy students interested in learning how to make and restore instruments
Contact: Hans E. Tausig, President

Warren (Riley J. & Lillian N.) and Beatrice W. Blanding Foundation
6 Ford Avenue
Oneonta, NY 13820
(607) 432–6720

Religious Denomination: Nondenominational
Field of Interest: Elementary parochial education
Amount Funded: $179,750
$ Given: $2,000 to $15,000
Contact: Henry L. Hulbert, Managing Trustee

Wien (Lawrence A.) Foundation, Inc.
c/o Wien, Malkin and Bettex
60 East 42nd Street
New York, NY 10165
(212) 687–8700

Religious Denomination: Jewish, Friends, Roman Catholic, United Methodist, Presbyterian, Protestant, and nondenominational
Field of Interest: Parochial education

NORTH CAROLINA

Blumenthal Foundation for Charity, Religion, Education, and Better Inter–Faith Relations
P.O. Box 34689
Charlotte, NC 28234–6080
(704) 377–6555

Religious Denomination: Jewish, Methodist, Baptist, Roman Catholic, Christian, United Methodist, Presbyterian, Lutheran, Salvation Army, and nondenominational
Field of Interest: Secondary parochial education
Amount Funded: $920,093
$ Given: Ranges from $100 to $1,000 and from $2,000 to $10,000
Contact: Herman Blumenthal, Trustee

OHIO

Anderson Foundation
P.O. Box 119
Maumee, OH 43537
(419) 891–6404

Religious Denomination: Roman Catholic, Protestant, Jewish, Presbyterian, Baptist, Lutheran, Mennonite, United Methodist, Hindu, United Church of Christ, Evangelical, and nondenominational
Field of Interest: Secondary education
Contact: Beverly Lange, Secretary to the Chairman

MISCELLANEOUS GRANTS

American Music Scholarship Association (AMSA)
1826 Carew Tower
Cincinnati, OH 45202
(513) 421–5342

Field of Interest: Piano performance
Amount Funded: $150,000
Description: Seeks to expose young pianists ages 5–30 to the influence of performances by great musicians; sponsors International Piano Competition; bestows awards
Contact: Gloria Ackerman, Executive Director

Gratzer (Helen) Charitable Foundation Trust
Society National Bank
800 Superior Avenue
Cleveland, OH 44114
(216) 689–3000

Religious Denomination: Evangelical, Lutheran, and Episcopal
Field of Interest: Elementary and secondary parochial education
Contact: T.J. Connons, Vice President

HCS Foundation
1235 Ohio Savings Plaza
1801 East 9th Street
Cleveland, OH 44114–3103
(216) 781–3502

Religious Denomination: Roman Catholic
Field of Interest: Secondary parochial education

National Forum for the Advancement of Aquatics
1753 Red Robin Road
Columbus, OH 43229
(614) 888–7712

Field of Interest: Aquatics
Description: Research and training grants for qualified students of aquatics
Contact: Connie Coughenhour, Chair

Sapirstein–Stone–White Foundation
10500 American Road
Cleveland, OH 44144
(216) 252–7300

Religious Denomination: Jewish
Field of Interest: Elementary and secondary parochial education
Amount Funded: $1,152,748
$ Given: $10,000 to $50,000
Contact: Mary Kay Incandela, Financial Administrator

Tell (Paul P.) Foundation, Inc.
1105 Trans Ohio Building
7 West Bowery Street
Akron, OH 44308
(216) 434–8355

Religious Denomination: Evangelical, nondenominational, interdenominational, Baptist, and Church of God
Field of Interest: Secondary parochial education
Contact: David J. Schipper, Executive Director

OKLAHOMA

Mu Alpha Theta
601 Elm, Room 423
Norman, OK 73019
(405) 325–4489

Field of Interest: Mathematics
Description: Awards to high school and junior college students

Warren (William K.) Foundation
P.O. Box 470372
Tulsa, OK 74147–0372
(918) 492–8100

Religious Denomination: Roman Catholic
Field of Interest: Secondary parochial education
Amount Funded: $14,505,025
$ Given: Ranges from $1,000 to $25,000 and from $50,000 to $200,000
Contact: W.R. Lissau, President

OREGON

Chiles Foundation
111 Southwest Fifth Avenue, Suite 4050
Portland, OR 97204
(503) 222–2143

Religious Denomination: Roman Catholic, United Methodist, Baptist, Episcopal
Field of Interest: Primary and secondary education
Contact: Walt Abel

San Felipe del Rio, Inc.
P.O. Box 21
Oakland, OR 97462
(503) 459–4474

Description: Minor support through scholarships to individuals
$ Given: $1,102 to $1,500
Contact: Robert P. Conte, Executive Director

MISCELLANEOUS GRANTS

PENNSYLVANIA

Charles G. Berwind Foundation
3000 Centre Southwest
1500 Market Street
Philadelphia, PA 19102
(215) 563–2800

Description: Occasional scholarships given to high school residents of area of corporate operation
Application Procedure: Deadline November 30; completion of formal application required
Contact: Betty A. Olund, Administrator

Connelly Foundation
9300 Aston Road
Philadelphia, PA 19136
(215) 698–5203

Religious Denomination: Roman Catholic
Field of Interest: Elementary and secondary parochial education
Contact: John F. Connelly, President

Charles E. Ellis Grant and Scholarship Fund
c/o Educational Advisory Services International
1101 Market, Suite 2850
Philadelphia, PA 19107
(215) 928–0900

Description: Scholarships to functionally orphaned female students who reside in Philadelphia County, PA, for high school–level education; scholarships not available for college–level education
Amount Funded: $1,061,305
Contact: Trust Administration Department

Huston Foundation
P.O. Box 139
Gladwyne, PA 19035
(215) 527–4371

Religious Denomination: Episcopal, Evangelical, Pentecostal, and Presbyterian
Field of Interest: Secondary parochial education
Contact: Nancy Hansen, Vice President

Kavanagh (T. James) Foundation
P.O. Box 609
Broomall, PA 19008
(215) 356–0743

Religious Denomination: Roman Catholic, United Methodist, Baptist, Episcopal, Presbyterian, and Salvation Army
Field of Interest: Elementary and secondary parochial education
Amount Funded: $157,853
$ Given: $1,000 to $5,000
Contact: Brenda S. Brooks, Chief Executive Officer

McShain (John) Charities, Inc.
540 N. 17th Street
Philadelphia, PA 19130
(215) 564–2322

Religious Denomination: Roman Catholic
Field of Interest: Secondary parochial education
Amount Funded: $2,355,619
$ Given: Ranges from $100 to $10,000 and from $50,000 to $100,000
Contact: John McShain, Foundation Director

A. Marlyn Moyer, Jr. Scholarship Foundation
P.O. Box 512
Southampton, PA 18966
(215) 943–7400

Description: Scholarships to residents of Bucks County, PA, who attend Bucks County high schools
Amount Funded: $22,500
$ Given: 16 grants to individuals, ranging from $1,000 to $2,000
Application Procedure: Write to Lower Bucks County Chamber of Commerce, 409 Hood Boulevard, Fairless Hills, PA 19030
Contact: Susan Harkins

Muller (C. John & Josephine) Foundation, Inc.
2800 Grant Avenue
Philadelphia, PA 19114
(215) 676–7576

Religious Denomination: Nondenominational
Field of Interest: Elementary and secondary parochial education
Amount Funded: $941,150
$ Given: $5,000 to $60,000
Contact: C. John Muller, Director

Stern (Harry) Family Foundation
c/o Mervin J. Hartmann
Three Parkway, 20th Floor
Philadelphia, PA 19102
(215) 563–0650

Religious Denomination: Jewish
Field of Interest: Parochial education
Contact: Jerome Stern, Secretary & Director

SOUTH CAROLINA

Bailey Foundation
P.O. Box 1276
Clinton, SC 29325
(803) 833–6830

Religious Denomination: Baptist, Church of God, Presbyterian, Episcopal, Pentecostal, United Methodist
Field of Interest: Primary and secondary education
Application Procedure: Apply between September and November
Contact: H. William Carter, Jr., Administrator

TENNESSEE

Bullard (George Newton) Foundation
c/o Sovran Bank/Central South
1 Commerce Place
Nashville, TN 37219
(615) 749–3259

Religious Denomination: Baptist, Christian, Evangelical, Methodist, Presbyterian
Field of Interest: Primary education
Contact: George Bullard, Jr., Trustee

Guzikowski Family Foundation
Sovran Bank/Central South
One Commerce Place
Nashville, TN 37219
(615) 749–3336

Religious Denomination: Roman Catholic
Field of Interest: Elementary and secondary parochial education
Amount Funded: $238,800
$ Given: $800 to $20,000
Contact: M. Kirk Scobey, Sr., Trust Officer

The Nehemiah Foundation
230 Wilson Pike Circle
P.O. Box 2036
Brentwood, TN 37027
(615) 373–1560

Description: Grants to parents for their children's education
$ Given: $16,727 in grants to individuals
Contact: William Z. Baumgartner, Jr., President

Westend Foundation, Inc.
c/o American National Bank and Trust Co.
736 Market Street
Chattanooga, TN 37402
(615) 265–8881

Description: Scholarships and grants generally to Chattanooga, TN area residents; scholarships for higher education awarded for study at colleges, universities, technical schools and medical schools; secondary school scholarships awarded to students attending preparatory schools in Chattanooga, TN; grants awarded to educational institutions for designated students
Amount Funded: $227,257
$ Given: 42 grants to individuals, totalling $61,500 and ranging from $750 to $3,000
Contact: Raymond B. Witt, Jr., Secretary

TEXAS

Beasley (Theodore & Beulah) Foundation, Inc.
3811 Turtle Creek Blvd., Suite 1370
Dallas, TX 75219–4419
(214) 522–8790

Religious Denomination: Christian and Episcopal
Contact: Sam Dashevsky, Vice President & Treasurer

Bosque Foundation
2911 Turtle Creek Blvd., Suite 1080
Dallas, TX 75219
(214) 559–0088

Religious Denomination: Methodist, Episcopal, Roman Catholic, Baptist
Field of Interest: Primary and secondary education
Contact: Louis A. Beecherl, Jr., Trustee

Brown Foundation
2118 Welch Avenue
P.O. Box 130646
Houston, TX 77219
(713) 523–6867

Religious Denomination: Presbyterian, Methodist, Baptist, Roman Catholic, Salvation Army, nondenominational
Field of Interest: Primary and secondary education
Contact: Katherine Dobelman, Executive Director

Cameron (Harry S. & Isabel C.) Foundation
c/o NCNC–Texas National Bank
P.O. Box 2518
Houston, TX 77252–2518
(713) 652–6526

Field of Interest: Primary and secondary education
Contact: Carl Schumaker, Administrator

CIOS
4515 Lake Shore Street
Waco, TX 76710
(817) 757–0174

Religious Denomination: Protestant, Baptist, Methodist, Congregational Christian Church, and Pentecostal
Field of Interest: Secondary parochial education
Amount Funded: $2,072,208
$ Given: $1,000 to $17,000
Contact: Paul P. Piper, Trustee

Doering (William & Louise) Charitable Foundation
10820 Bushire
Dallas, TX 75229

Description: Scholarships to students attending four Christian day schools: Our Redeemer Lutheran School; Lutheran High School of Dallas, Texas; St. John's Lutheran School, Galveston, Texas; First Lutheran School, Ponca City, Oklahoma
$ Given: $750 to $1,500

Dougherty (James R.), Jr. Foundation
Box 640
Beeville, TX 18104
(512) 358–3560

Religious Denomination: Roman Catholic, nondenominational, Episcopal, and Baptist
Field of Interest: Secondary parochial education
Contact: Hugh Grove, Jr.

Fair (R.W.) Foundation
P.O. Box 689
Tyler, TX 75710
(314) 592–3811

Religious Denomination: United Methodist, Baptist, Presbyterian, Jewish, and Roman Catholic
Field of Interest: Elementary parochial education
Contact: Wilton H. Fair, President

Kenedy (John G. & Marie Stella) Memorial Foundation
First City Tower II, Ste. 1020
Corpus Christi, TX 78478
(512) 887–6565

Religious Denomination: Roman Catholic
Field of Interest: Elementary and secondary parochial education
Contact: James R. McCown, General Manager

Mays Foundation
914 S. Tyler Street
Amarillo, TX 79101
(806) 376–5417

Religious Denomination: Baptist and Evangelical
Field of Interest: Elementary and secondary parochial education
Amount Funded: $75,861
$ Given: $100 to $3,000
Contact: Troy M. Mays, Trustee

National Athletic Trainers Association
2952 Stemmons Freeway
Suite 200
Dallas, TX 75247–6103
(214) 637–6282

Field of Interest: Athletic training
Description: Awards and scholarships for athletic training in universities & colleges, high schools, preparatory schools, and military establishments

O'Connor (Kathryn) Foundation
One O'Connor Plaza
Suite 1100
Victoria, TX 77901
(512) 578–6271

Religious Denomination: Roman Catholic
Field of Interest: Elementary and secondary parochial education
Amount Funded: $377,684
$ Given: $5,000 to $20,000
Contact: Dennis O'Connor, President

VIRGINIA

Foundation for Exceptional Children
1920 Association Drive
Reston, VA 22091
(703) 620–1054

Field of Interest: Education for the gifted/disabled
Description: Scholarships and small grants to institutions, agencies, educators, parents and other persons concerned with the education and personal welfare of gifted or disabled children
Contact: Robert L. Silber, Executive Director

Morgan (Marietta M. & Samuel T.), Jr. Trust
c/o Scorran Bank
P.O. Box 26903
Richmond, VA 23261
(804) 788–2963

Religious Denomination: Christian
Field of Interest: Elementary and secondary parochial education
Amount Funded: $384,160
$ Given: $5,000 to $25,000
Contact: Elizabeth D. Seaman, Consultant

WASHINGTON

Stewardship Foundation
P.O. Box 1278
Tacoma, WA 98401
(206) 272–8336

Religious Denomination: Evangelical, nondenominational, Roman Catholic, Episcopal, Baptist, interdenominational, Lutheran, and Presbyterian
Field of Interest: Elementary and secondary parochial education
Amount Funded: $3,548,492
$ Given: $1,000 to $10,000
Contact: George Kovats, Executive Director

WISCONSIN

Carrie Foundation
1 East Milwaukee Street
Janesville, WI 53545
(608) 756–4141

Religious Denomination: Roman Catholic
Field of Interest: Secondary parochial education
Amount Funded: $172,300
$ Given: Ranges from $200 to $500 and from $5,000 to $25,000
Contact: George K. Steil, Sr., Trustee

DeRance Foundation
7700 W. Blue Mound Road
Wauwatosa, WI 53213
(414) 475–7700

Religious Denomination: Roman Catholic
Field of Interest: Elementary and secondary parochial education
Contact: Donald A. Gallagher, Executive Vice President

Phillips (L.E.) Family Foundation
3925 N. Hastings Way
Eau Claire, WI 54703
(715) 839–2139

Religious Denomination: Jewish, Lutheran, Salvation Army, Roman Catholic, United Methodist, nondenominational, and United Church of Christ
Field of Interest: Secondary parochial education
Amount Funded: $2,596,753
$ Given: Ranges from $100 to $1,000 and from $2,000 to $10,000
Contact: Eileen Cohen, Director

Index

N

O

X

Y

Books in Laurie Blum's **Free Money** Series

. . . .

THE FREE MONEY FOR CHILD CARE SERIES

Free Money for Day Care

- Advice on finding financial aid for family day care, child care centers, in-house care, and camp and summer programs

Free Money for Private Schools

- Where to find money for preschool and nursery education, private primary schools, and private secondary schools

Free Money for Children's Medical and Dental Care

- Ways to receive money for both long- and short-term medical care, dental and orthodontic treatment, and dermatological procedures

Free Money for Behavioral and Genetic Childhood Disorders

- Free Money for treatment of learning disabilities, eating disorders, retardation, alcohol and drug abuse, neurological disturbances, and sleep disorders

THE FREE MONEY FOR HEALTH CARE SERIES

Free Money for Diseases of Aging

- Find money to help pay for major surgery and medical care for diseases of aging such as Alzheimer's, Parkinson's, stroke, and other chronic illnesses

Free Money for Heart Disease and Cancer Care

- Ways to receive money for the diagnosis and treatment (surgery or long-term care) of cancer and heart disease

Free Money for Fertility Treatments

- Where to look for Free Money for infertility testing, treatment, insemination, and preliminary adoption expenses

Free Money for the Care and Treatment of Mental and Emotional Disorders

- Detailed guidance on locating Free Money for psychological care